₹ 21-

Summer Showers
in
Brindavan
1990

Discourses of

BHAGAVAN SRI SATHYA SAI BABA
during the Summer Course held at
Brindavan, Whitefield, Bangalore
on

Indian Culture and Spirituality

PRASANTHI NILAYAM

SRI SATHYA SAI BOOKS AND PUBLICATIONS TRUST,
PRASANTHI NILAYAM, ANANTAPUR DISTRICT,
ANDHRA PRADESH 515134, INDIA

INTERNATIONAL STANDARD BOOK NUMBER 81-7208-057-3
81-7208-113-8 (SET)

Published in India by:

The Convenor, Sri Sathya Sai Books and Publications Trust,
Prasanthi Nilayam, India — Pin Code 515 134.

Price: Rs.14.00

Printed by: Sharada Press, Mangalore.

Bhagavan Sri Sathya Sai Baba

CONTENTS

1. The Glory of Indian Culture 1

2. Sanctify the body 11

3. The Moving Temple 24

4. Mastery of the Senses 39

5. Road to Divinity 55

6. Hold the Reins 69

7. Vagaries of the Mind 78

8. Buddhi the Charioteer 88

9. Egoism and Attachment 98

10. The Three Gunas 105

11. Know Thyself 115

12. Self-knowledge 124

13. What is Freedom 129

14. Practice and Precept 146

15. Ascent of Man 155

16. Vedic Wisdom 163

17. Book List 174

The Glory of Indian Culture

The entire Cosmos has emerged from Truth
And it will merge back in Truth
Where is the place beyond the sway of Truth?
Behold, brothers, That which is the Pure Satwa!

Embodiments of Divine Love, dear students, teachers and patrons of education!

To every man born on earth, Truth is verily the visible God. The entire universe consisting of movable and immovable objects has emerged from Truth. Sathyam-Jnanam-Anantam-Brahma. Truth is indeed Brahman. Truth is endless. According to Vedantins, Truth is synonymous with the eternal Brahman. Hence Truth alone has to be revered by everyone. Bharatiyas - Indians are wedded to Truth and Righteousness. Justice is their mainstay. Every man is the inheritor of Truth and Righteousness. Young boys and girls who want to promote peace and harmony should strive to seek and pursue Truth. Bharatiyas cherish the welfare of the world. Our youth should therefore dedicate themselves to universal well-being. This is our creed or religion, so to speak. It is because we have forgotten such sacred Truth as well as our culture and the sanctity thereof, that we are unable to achieve communal unity and national integrity.

Truth and Righteousness will never submit to anything. All kinds of power, whether physical, intellectual, monetary, military or political, have to bend before Truth and Righteousness; but the latter will yield to none. Truth and Righteousness will always triumph.

The chief requisite of man's life is to be human. Whatever be our scholarship or position of authority, we

1

should not ignore the human values. Indian culture is unparalleled and most wonderful. Having forgotten the grandeur and glory of their heritage, the students of to-day enticed by so-called modernity, have become oblivious to their own innate divinity. The whirlwind of the rapidly progressing science and technology coupled with industrialisation is bringing about undesirable changes in our society by way of uprooting the moral or ethical values so essential for human well-being. Science and technology have, no doubt, contributed substantially to material progress but they have altogether undermined spiritual values such as selflessness, divinity and dignity inherent in man. In a way they have devalued humanity itself so much so that the present generation of young men and women are unable to recognise their divine nature. They are considering selfcentredness as the goal of life. Demonic qualities like ostentation, egoism, excessive and empty talk are playing their devil dance in society. This very country which has been the spiritual teacher of entire mankind is becoming the playfield of evil forces like injustice, indiscipline, licentiousness and defiance of Truth. Having become slaves to modernity, people are utterly disregarding Truth and Righteousness, and ignoring the hoary Indian culture and traditions, with the false notion that material self advancement is the *summun bonum* of life. What the students have to protect today is not the nation. They have to safeguard Truth and Righteousness only. These two, in turn will protect the nation. Giving up Truth and Righteousness, educated persons now-a-days are causing damage to the nation, ostensibly in the name of protecting it.

People do not become wise by mere education. They are considering education as a means of livelihood rather than the art of living. The supreme goal of life should ever be kept in view. A small piece of fertile land is more valuable than a large tract of barren land; so also character is much more valuable and essential than scholarship. Today everybody is striving to acquire wealth, power and pelf which are like passing clouds while nobody bothers himself to acquire virtues which lead to the Truth Eternal. You must try to become exemplars of virtues, but not of wealth and power. It is a pity that even the elders who profess themselves to be well-wishers of society, are giving up their own ancient culture, lured by modernity. When the mother cow is grazing off the crop in the field, will its calf stand quiet on the field bund? It is impossible. It is no wonder the younger generation is following the bad example of their elders, leaders, parents and teachers who are not setting the right example for the youth to emulate. What is the reason for our ancients earning name and fame as upholders of morality in society? Because of their exemplary practice of virtues in daily life. They pursued the four Purusharthas - goals of life - scrupulously and shared with others benefits and joys derived therefrom. But the present day youngsters are groping in the dark, aimlessly indulging in all sorts of indiscriminate activities.

Dharma - Right Conduct, Artha - Wealth, Kama - Desire and Moksha - Liberation are the four Purusharthas - goals of human life. Dispensing with Dharma which is like the feet, and Moksha which may be compared to the head, people are hankering after Artha and Kama only, resulting in disorder and insecurity in the society and nation in general. The root cause for loss of peace and security is the neglect of Truth and Righteousness, which are highly indispensable for man.

3

Students ! Do not forget our ancient culture, which is the very life-breath of Bharatiyas. Bharat had offered the gems of its great culture to the world at large in the past. The nation has suffered a serious set-back due to the ever-growing malady of aping other countries. Imitation is human, Creation is Divine. The right education for the students is the manifestation of their innate divinity.

About fifty years, back, the youth of our country, imbued with patriotism and love for our culture, used to follow the footsteps of the elders. The national leaders, teachers and scholars of those days were setting up exemplary ideals. There was harmony in their thoughts, words and deeds. That is why the younger generation was following their example. They used to decorate their rooms with pictures of divine incarnations and national leaders whom they used to adore and emulate. However it is a matter for regret that now-a-days either ideal teachers or ideal leaders are conspicuous by their absence. They say something and actually do something else, with the result that they have forfeited the confidence of the young. Today the pictures of their favourite film stars adorn the walls of the students' rooms. What is the reason for this degeneration of their minds? The only reason is the dearth of ideal leaders who believe, practise and propagate the Indian culture. Nevertheless, Bharatiya culture might be seen by the discerning eye, to be pervading not only the manner of dressing and speaking, working and playing but also every activity undertaken from dawn to dusk.

In present day India there are many persons who do not understand what Samskriti - culture is. There can be no human life without Samskriti. It is a way of life. Ignoring this way and taking to wrong

4

paths, men are losing peace and security. Everyone wants comfort. But no attempt is being made to recognise what real comfort is. Eating four times a day, sleeping, viewing television and films three or four times, forgetful of the outside world - these are considered to contribute to comfort or happiness. Among all living creatures, to be born as a human being is declared by the scriptures as a rare privilege. But if man too is content merely with eating, drinking, mating and sleeping like birds and beasts, without trying to understand what Samskriti is, his life is a sheer waste.

The word Samskriti originating from Samskritam refers to the process of refinement of every object before it is made fit for human use. For example, consider how many transformations are undergone by paddy before it becomes fit for human consumption - thrashing the paddy grains from the sheaves, winnowing and separating grains from chaff, pounding or milling to remove the husk from the grain, cleaning the rice by removing extraneous matter like small stones and weed seeds etc. soaking the raw rice in water and finally cooking over fire to get cooked rice. Such Samskriti - refinement also enhances the value of things. For instance, the value of paddy is, say, one hundred rupees per bag. But, when it is dehusked and cleaned in the milling process, the value of one bag of rice will be six hundred rupees - sixfold increase due to refinement. Let us consider a second example. If a wrist watch made of stainless steel is crushed and thrown into fire, the resulting mass of stainless steel will not be worth even a quarter of a rupee. But the same mass of steel when fabricated into a wrist watch by the manufacturing process, its worth is enhanced to one thousand rupees. To give another illustration, cotton harvested from the

5

cotton plant has to be dried, the unwanted calyx removed, and then put in a ginning machine to separate the seeds from the lint; the lint has to be spun into yarn in a spinning machine; and the yarn has to be woven into cloth in a weaving mill. Thus when cotton is transformed into cloth, its value and utility are enhanced. Likewise, man should not remain in the state in which he was born. He should manifest his inherent divinity. Students should therefore try to acquire, in addition to academic knowledge, qualities like humility and discrimination, which will help them to become full-fledged human personalities. As a seed finds fulfilment in a fruit-bearing tree, man should find fulfilment in a purposeful life leading to perfection through Samskarana-transformation, and yielding the fruits of peace, security and love.

Love is a divine quality in man. But it should be shown not only towards other human beings, but also towards birds, beasts and other living creatures. True Samskriti lies in such an expansion of love, giving up narrowness and developing broad-mindedness which results in real joy for oneself and for the society as well. Thus will human nature be sublimated into divinity.

The Vedas which are the repositories of Indian Culture have declared that one should not entertain hatred or illwill towards any living being. Therefore along with their normal studies, the students should acquaint themselves with the Indian Culture and put it into practice.

You are all aware how in the present day world man is losing foresight in every thought, sacrificing Truth in every word and forsaking righteousness in every

6

action. Love is on the decline on all fronts and progressive ideas are given the go-by. Spirituality is being ridiculed. Hatred based on caste and religion is ever on the increase. Parochialism and selfishness are running riot and playing havoc. If today revolutions are rampant, what is the reason for it? It is because people have forsaken fear of sin, love for God and morality in society. There is no benefit to the world from people who have the human form sans discrimination and discipline which are the characteristics of a true man. Students! Along with your usual education you must imbibe the qualities of faith in the nation to which you belong, and cherishing the welfare of the world in which you live. Since ancient times, it has been the Hindu tradition to pray for the happiness of all. Bharat has been contributing to the stability, peace and security of all nations through its unique spiritual genius.

The Vedas which are the basis for Indian Culture have taught, speak truth - practice righteousness. Unfortunately today people do not speak truth. They talk about right-eousness but do not practise it. If we protect Dharma, practising it, Dharma in turn will protect us. Dharma does not mean the mere observance of certain traditions and formalities. It is the harmony of thought, word and deed, which results in the purification of these faculties. Today Dharma has declined because of the lack of such harmony and purity of the Trikaranas- three instruments of action. The Upanishads exhort man not to abandon Sathya - Truth and Dharma - Righteousness under any circumstances even at the risk of his life; King Harishchandra stands out as the supreme exemplar in this respect.

Truth alone triumphs. One who wants to achieve victory should follow Dharma. Dhritarashtra asked Sanjaya, "in your opinion, who will win the Kurukshetra war -

Pandavas or Kauravas?" Sanjaya, who was the master of his senses, replied, "O King! Where there is the Almighty Lord together with the virtuous Arjuna devoted to truth and righteousness, there certainly will victory be". There is no Dharma or religion higher than Sathya - Truth. Dharma depends on Sathya. Bhagavata declares that there is no greater sin than going back on one's own plighted word. Hence Sathya is supreme. Sathya and Dharma are inter-dependent and inseparable.

Boys and girls - children of Bharath! The path of truth is supremely important. We should firmly believe that it is the Divine Principle and pay obeisance to it accordingly. People study and learn about various things, but, with all their education they do not know their own Reality. The more one's book-learning, the more argumentative one becomes. Howsoever educated a wicked fellow might be, his evil nature will not change. What is the use of straining oneself to acquire such worthless education? That alone is true education which confers immortality on man. That is indeed the education in Truth and Righteousness. Sathya and Dharma are inseparable from the virtuous and noble persons. That is why Truth which is eternal is also called as Atma, which is the core of all beings. While all other objects and beings are subject to change like the passing clouds, it is Atma alone that remains changeless. That does not mean that you should give up secular learning. Along with it you should try to acquire the knowledge of that which is real and everlasting. How many have not acquired high educational qualifications, name and fame? But how transient and fleeting are such things! The body itself is impermanent. However, even when the body perishes, our Samskaras - accumulated mental impressions will remain with us permanently. We should remember that we should live not for the sake of Annam - food, but for the sake of Adarsham - ideal. Ideals are always supreme and everlasting. If one person becomes an ideal, he can influence the lives of many others for the better. It is better to live like the swan for one year than to live like the crow for hundred years. It is enough if you live even for ten years as ideal students. To lead an ideal life, it is essential to have love of the nation and love of the Spirit - Atma, as well as love and respect for parents.

Students! Try to recognise how sacred, how pure, how exemplary, how loving, how sublime, and how vast your motherland is. Many young men of India are now-a-days going abroad, belittling their own motherland as worthless. In fact, no other country in the world has really all the worthwhile things that Bharat has. Born in this land of Karma, Yoga and Thyaga, students should understand and cherish its cultural heritage. Their present ignorance of this sacred culture is due to the absence of teachers and parents who could convey the elements of this culture to the students. During the fifteen days of this Summer Course, you, students should learn how to harmonise our ancient culture and tradition with the needs of the modern world and to lead lives governed by Truth and Righteousness. Position or Power is not important. They are transient like the passing clouds. One should not be proud of one's wealth, progeny or youthful vigour. They may all disappear in a moment. Adolescence is a very precious period in one's life. It should be rightly used. Once you waste this precious period, you cannot get it back later on, strive as you may, with all your effort. Try to develop faith in the sacred Bharatiya Culture which transcends the limitations of time, space and circumstances. During these fifteen days, endeavour to understand fully the glory and unique greatness of our culture.

In his welcome address, the Vice-Chancellor Sri Saraf prayed that I should explain to you the functions and significance of the body, senses, mind, intellect and Atma. It is essential for students to know about these matters. Of what avail is it for one to know all about the external world without knowing abut one's own reality! It is important for you to understand the nature of Brahman - the supreme Oversoul, and Atman - the individual soul. This is the royal path to the fulfilment of human life. Students - both boys and girls, should sanctify this precious period of time by imbibing sacred ideas and ideals, and then strive to spread the same throughout the the length and breadth of this vast country of ours. Do not forget that in all these matters, devotion is the most important requisite. Without divine Grace we cannot achieve anything. For anyone to think that he can achieve things by himself is only to betray his egoistic arrogance. Therefore, try to develop faith in Atma-Self, and then you can achieve everything.

Sanctify the Body

You are not the body, a bundle of flesh,
blood and bones;
Neither are you the unmanifested desires,
nor the manifested mind;
You are not also the infatuating delusion
that thwarts your liberation;
But you are the Eternal Paramatman,
if only you recognise your innate power.

Students! Embodiments of Divine Love!

The body, the senses, the mind and the intellect are only the vestures put on by man. Only when we understand the nature and significance of these adjuncts, can we make proper use of them. You wear trousers, banian, shirt and coat. Only when you know how to use each of these things correctly, can you use them in the proper way and get the benefit therefrom. Otherwise you may make bizarre use of them, like putting on the banian over the shirt or wearing the pant in the reverse direction. Hence you generally ensure that you wear your daily attire correctly so as to give a decent and attractive appearance. Likewise the body is our garment. It is only when we know how to wear it and use it appropriately that we can make good use of it and get the best out of it.

Dahyati iti dehah - That which is burnt is called the body. This is the derivative meaning of the word Deha - body. It is a matter of common knowledge that the body is burnt after death. But even when it is alive, the body experiences burning due to worries. The body is inert. It is a storehouse of filth and subject to all kinds of diseases.

11

It is a bundle of bones and flesh and cannot help you to cross the ocean of births and deaths. So, Oh Mind! instead of relying on such a flimsy body, better cling to the Lotus Feet of Lord Hari. This was the prayer of the sages. The body which is made up of the five elements is impermanent. But you who have put on this body are verily the supreme God who is eternal and unchanging. It is therefore, up to you to use your power of discrimination in using the body wisely and thereby to derive joy from it.

Sarira is another name for the body. *Siryathe iti sariraha*. That which is liable to decay is called Sarira. At the time of birth, the body is a lump of flesh and blood. As it grows it attains beauty and enters the stage of adolescence and adulthood, when it becomes puffed up with the pride of beauty and vigour etc. In due course it is overtaken by the ravages of old age, resulting in loss of vitality and susceptibility to diseases. Thus the body is subject to many a change.

Yet another name for the body is Mandir - shrine or temple, because it enshrines the Jiva - individual soul, which in fact is no other than the eternal God-Supreme soul. Being the sacred and holy abode of God, the body should therefore, be not misused but utilised for entertaining good thoughts, for speaking good words and for performing good actions. Hence to facilitate such right use of the body, it should be kept in good trim.

Any instrument should be maintained in a fit condition, if it is to give satisfactory performance. For instance, you can write comfortably with a fountain pen only if it is filled with the required ink and when the nib also is in good condition. So also a knife can be used for cutting provided it has the required sharpness and suitable handle etc. Likewise the body which is an instrument to perform righteous actions should be kept in a suitable condition for that purpose. You can use a knife for cutting vegetables, fruits etc., but not for cutting a piece of iron. So also we should use the body with discrimination to achieve the purpose for which it is meant. Every time before you do anything, you should ask yourself - I am the Brahman dwelling in this body as the individual Atman. As such, is it proper for me to do this action or not? Only then will you be using the body in the right manner. Just because you have this body, you should not use it according to your whims and fancies, forgetting the fact that it is the temple of God, which should, therefore, be used for sacred purposes.

The body has also been called Kshetra. The one who congnises this Kshetra is the Kshetrajna - the knower of the Kshetra. You are the knower of the Kshetra and the body is the Kshetra which is known by you. Hence you are the witness of this body. Kshetra means a sacred place associated with the Divine and filled with holy vibrations, as for instance the places of pilgrimage like Kasi - Varanasi, Tirupati, Badri etc. These Kshetras are meant to be used for the performance of worship, redeeming religious vows, giving charity and such other sacred activities. Similarly, in the Kshetra of the body good thoughts and good actions alone should prevail. This is the inner meaning of the appellation Kshetra used for the body.

Another meaning of the term Kshetra is field. In this field of the body, the fruits we reap are dependent on the seeds we sow. If we sow good thoughts, we can harvest good fruits. Bad thoughts will only yield bad results. The body is thus a field in which the seeds of Punya - merit

13

and Papa - sin, are sown. We should, however, remember that the body as a field has certain advantages when compared to an agricultural field. In cultivating a field for raising crops, we have to wait for the right season and the optimum conditions to sow a particular variety of crop. The suitability of a land for growing a particular crop has to be taken into consideration. Sowing cannot be done indiscriminately. However in the case of the field of our body, there are no such constraints. It can be cultivated in all conditions and at all times including night and day. When you sow seeds on an arable land, you may get a good crop or poor crop. You may not realise your expectations. But in the case of the Human body, you are bound to reap the fruits of the good or bad thoughts and actions which you sow as seeds. You are sure to have cent percent return. As you sow, so you reap. This is an immutable law. You must therefore ensure that only seeds in the form of good thoughts and deeds are sown. You should not misuse the body as you like. You should discriminate between the transient and the permanent and utilise your body for achieving the ultimate good.

Those who wish to use the body properly and ensure that they entertain good thoughts, perform good acts and reap good results should scrupulously follow two things, viz., regulation of diet and regulation of other living habits. You should not consume any and every type of food merely to appease hunger or the palate. You must eat only Satwic food. Our thoughts are determined by the kind of food we consume. For instance, as is the firewood so is the fire as well as the smoke; if you use sandal wood, you will get the fragrant smoke; if you make use of a foul-smelling kind of fuel, you will get a foul-smelling smoke. Thus the kind of smoke depends on the kind of fire; again as is the smoke, so is the cloud; as is the cloud, so is the water; as is the water, so is the rain; as is the rain, so is the crop; as is the crop, so is the food; as is the food, so is the head - thoughts. Our thoughts, therefore, are the result of the type of food we eat. The body is cleansed by water, while the mind is purified by Truth. It is only when we take food that is conducive to truth that we can pursue the path of truth. As the body is a sacred shrine, you should strictly avoid taking any intoxicating substances. Articles of food that promote Rajasic qualities - which inflame passions, should be eschewed.

What is the meaning of Satwic food? The prevalent notion is that fruits and milk constitute Satwic food. But that is not all to it. What is consumed by the mouth is not the only food that enters the body. The other sense organs like the eyes, the ears, the nose and the hands also consume objects from the external world. Hence, just because a person takes fruits and milk through one of the five sense organs, he cannot claim to have taken Satwic food, unless the food taken by him through all the five senses is Satwic in nature. Through the eyes you have to see only what is pure. To see all kinds of things indiscriminately will spell disaster. The power of sight should be used only for sacred purposes. Unfortunately, however, the vision of youth today is getting increasingly perverted like Keechaka Drishti - lustful vision. The result is that they will meet with the same fate as Keechaka of the Mahabharatha, who was destroyed by Bhima. Students should be particularly careful in this regard. It is only when they use their eyes in a pure and sacred way will they be receiving Satwic impressions through the eyes.

The ears too need pure food. This means we should listen only to sacred words and to accounts relating to the Divine. Let us always hear good and pleasant things about others. In this way, we must safeguard the ears from being polluted by hearing bad things. Only thus can we ensure consuming Satwic food through the ears.

Only fragrant sweet-smelling scents should be absorbed through the nose. Inhaling bad odours will result in disease. If you inhale foul air, you will be breathing in disease producing organisms. You must inhale pure air, in a clean open space.

The hand also should be used to consume pure food. In other words, you must perform only good acts with your hands, befitting the appellation of temple, used for the body.

When you get rid of the five evils associated with the pollution of speech, sight, hearing, thought and action, you will be able to realise your own Divinity and become Paramatma - Supreme Soul. If the senses are fed with polluted food, you cannot become pure merely by taking milk and fruit. You must partake of pure Satwic food through all the five sense organs.

Usually a temple will have many gates. These gateways are intended to let in only devotees who seek to worship the deity inside the temple, but not all and sundry. Similarly for this temple of the body there are five gates. What is the purpose of these doorways? If we build a house and erect doors in it, they are intended to let in our kith and kin only and not all stray animals like dogs, pigs and donkeys etc. If such unwanted animals try to enter, the doors are shut against them. Likewise, the doors of the five senses in this sacred body should be kept open for sacred and divine entrants alone. Only then will it deserve the name Kshetra or Mandir. On the other hand, if unholy objects and ideas are allowed to enter, it ceases to be a holy temple. Thus it may be seen that Satwic food is very essential for putting the body to proper use.

Next comes Vihara - movement or association with places, persons, objects etc. You must consider seriously what sort of places you may visit, what kind of environment in which you should live and what type of persons with whom you ought to associate yourselves. Tell me your company and I shall tell you what you are, goes the adage. You should eschew all bad company, because your thoughts are influenced by the company you keep. Young people today are readily cultivating evil company. They take easily to bad ways. This amounts to belittling and devaluating the human body, which the scriptures have declared to be the most precious and rare possession among all created beings. Realising this fact the sages of yore chose to live in solitude in order to engage themselves in sacred thoughts and actions like devotional singing, meditation and penance. But even this may be considered as a sign of weakness, in a way. For instance, if you want to subdue anger, can you do it by retiring into a forest and doing austerities for any number of years? As your anger arises in the midst of people, it has to be conquered only in the same milieu and not in unpeopled forest. You may remain tranquil as long as you are in the forest, but when you come back to a crowd, you will be the same old irate person. If you want to control your senses, it is a delusion to imagine that you can do so by resorting to religious penance. It can be achieved easily if you understand the subtle workings of the body, but not by any other means. Suppose you buy a new car, you must know how to drive it properly. Just because you have purchased it with your own money and got it duly registered, you cannot sit at the steering wheel and drive as you like, for it would then be dangerous to your car, to yourself and to the public as well. Although the car may be yours, you must know how to use it properly. It should be noted that all the problems and troubles of man are due to the fact that he does not know how to make proper use of his body. Hence he becomes an easy prey to sorrow and disease. One thing should always be remembered. No one can go against the Divine Will. No one can alter the Lord's Law which is immutable.

The body in inert. Many may argue as to how the body can be called inert, when it is seen to be capable of growth. The answer to this doubt is that when you clean your house daily and go on dumping the sweepings in one place, it will grow into a big heap. Likewise, when you go on dumping into your body various kinds of food so many times per day, your body, though insentient, will grow like the heap of garbage. It should however be realised that the body is able to function by way of eating, talking, walking and growing etc., because of the Chaithanya - Consciousness within it. In this respect the body may be compared to a car. Eyes are like the headlights, tongue like the horn and ears like the loud-speakers. It is because of the battery inside the car that the above-mentioned parts of the car are also able to function. Similarly, the various organs of the inert body are able to function only because of the Atmic Power inside the body. To cite another anology, the inert iron filings are able to move hither and thither when attracted by the power of a magnet. So also, the operation of all the organs of the body, which are inert by themselves is made possible by the presence of the Atma inside. It is a pity that we spend a lot of time, effort and money to beautify the transient and inert body, forgetting our real Atma, Self which is permanent and sentient.

Man is prone to three kinds of misconceptions in relation to his body. One is to mistake himself to be something which is not his real Self. Another is to regard persons or objects that do not belong to him as his own. The third is to believe the evanescent to be the everlasting. Man considers the body as his real self. If that is the case, why should he say, this is my body. This statement clearly implies that he is different from the body, because the owner is different from what he owns. For instance, when a man says, this is my kerchief, he is apart from the kerchief. Hence, how can one say that he is the body? This is the first and basic blunder.

Secondly, in worldly matters man is misled by the belief that he is the owner of various kinds of properties like houses, lands, vehicles etc. You build a house and call it yours. When you sell it, it is no longer yours. Likewise, you buy a car and call it yours. When it is sold, it ceases to be yours. So, things are yours only as long as you own and use them. Forgetting that all these possessions are temporary like fleeting clouds, you develop undue attachments for them. In fact, nothing is yours. How can those which belong to the body be yours? All these misconceptions are caused by the veil of Maya - delusion and the resultant sense of possessiveness and the aberrations of the mind. Prior to marriage, no one can say who is the husband and who is the wife. Before birth, nobody can say who is the mother and who is the child. Only after marriage, you say this is my wife. It is only after birth, you declare - he is my son. But these relationships are transient and not permement and are based on the wrong indentification of oneself with the body. Nobody brings with him even a tiny piece of cloth at the time of birth, and nobody leaves his address even, at the time death. If they are really yours, why won't they give you their address at the time of final departure? Nothing belongs to you. Forgetting your own reality and mistaking the unreal as the real in this illusory world, you are creating problems for yourself. You are always yourself only. You don't belong to anybody, nor does anyone belong to you. There is only one thing that exists. Despite the unequivocal declaration of the scriptures that Reality is One, but sages call it differently - we continue to believe wrongly that diversity is real.

Let us consider the case of the head of a household or family. His wife calls him - My dear husband. His son calls him - My dear father. His mother calls him - My dear son, while his daughter-in-law refers to him as - My dear father-in-law. Thus one and the same person is called in different ways according to various relationships with the body. As the scriptures declare - the One has become many. Therefore, there is unity underlying the diversity. There is only One. That one is the Hero - God; all the rest - i.e., the entire world, is zero. When you put one zero by the side of that one, it becomes ten; with one more zero it becomes hundred, and with a third zero, it becomes one thousand, and so on. Wherefrom do all these zeros get their value? It is only from the Hero. If you remove the Hero, there is no value for any number of zeroes. Therefore, God alone is the Hero. The delusions of the body, mind, intellect etc. are only zeroes. So, it is important that we should hold on to the Hero - God. That does not mean that you should give up the world or abandon your wordly duties.

You have to do your duty by your kith and kin. But while thus discharging your duties, you should never deviate from the spiritual path. Your secular life should be harmonised with your spiritual life. So long as you live in the world, you have to conform to the rules and regulations governing the worldly affairs. But whatever you may do, you must not lose sight of the Supreme - spiritual goal of life. You should recognise the fact that nothing belongs to you whether mother, father, brother, kinsmen, wealth, house etc. All these ephemeral things are related to the changing body which is the basis for all mental aberrations.

The body undergoes various changes due to food and other living habits. Whatever be such changes in the body, the individuality remains unchanged. The changes of name and form such as childhood, boyhood, manhood and old age pertain to the body and hence illusory. You should not therefore consider the body as real and permanent at all. Neverthless it is your duty to ensure that the body is not subjected to diseases and is maintained as a fit instrument. As long as you sail in this river of life, you must see to it that the boat of your body does not develop holes or leaks thereby preventing water from entering into the boat. The boat may be in water, but there should be no water in the boat. Remain in the world and attend to your duties, but don't allow worries to enter your mind and make your body susceptible to all kinds of diseases. Consider the body as only an instrument.

To keep this instrument of the body in good trim, you have to regulate your food and other habits. Also, look upon the body as your vesture or clothing, and resort to washing it clean from time to time, just as soiled clothes are cleaned by the washerman. All that the washerman does is to remove the dirt from the cloth enabling it to regain its original whiteness. So too, purity is natural to the human body, but it becomes dirty due to improper use, and therefore you should get it cleaned

21

with the help of God as washerman, by resorting to such practices as prayer, japa, meditation and love of God. The washerman alone can wash the clothes, but not a barber. So also, God alone - and none else - can cleanse your heart of its impurities. Never forget that this body is only a garment. It is due to the ignorance that you look upon the body as your real Self. Only when you get rid of this ignorance, will you shine as the effulgent Sun of Wisdom.

Students! Besides the body, you have to recognise the role and importance of the other related entities like the sense organs, mind and intellect and keep them in good shape. If you keep Laddu - an Indian Sweet, or cloves in your shirt pocket and forgetfully give the shirt to the washerman, you will find that the pocket has developed stains when the washerman brings your shirt back to you after washing. Likewise the mind is stained with bad impressions if you allow bad thoughts to enter it. It is only when the nature of each of these constituents of your personality, viz., body, senses, mind and intellect is properly understood will you be able to lead an integral and purposeful human life. Otherwise you will become a victim of all sorts of difficulties and problems. You need not waste your time in the routine spiritual practices like Japa and Dhyana - meditation. To recognise the Truth is the real Sadhana. When food is cooked, there will be no longer any need for firewood. Likewise when Truth has been realised, there is no need for Sadhana.

During this fortnight if you are able to grasp the nature and significance of the body, the senses, the mind, the intellect and also the Atma- God, which is the Supreme witness presiding over the rest of them, you will be in a position to master the mystery of the Cosmos made up of the five basic elements - Pancha Bhutas. Ultimately, as God is the basis of everything, students have to develop faith in God.

The Moving Temple

This body is a valueless iron safe;
Like the precious jewels kept in an iron safe,
There is the Divine inside the body.
This Sai's word is the path of Truth.

What you call God is not in some far. off place,
That God is in your very body;
What you call sin is not in a distant country
It is there in the very actions that you perform.

Embodiments of the Divine Atma!

Although the human body is worthless in itself and is impermanent, it has to be carefully looked after, because it enshrines the Divine Atma. This is man's primary duty. Without a healthy and strong body, man will fall an easy victim to numerous ailments. Body is verily the foundation for human life. That is why the ancient Romans who were aware of this truth and who were the pioneers of modern civilisation in the West, used to carefully undertake various measures for the proper up-keep and development of the body.

The body is a world in itself. It is not merely the outer form. It is the collective assemblage of many organs and limbs. Each organ has its own beauty, which has to be fostered. A weak and unhealthy body is incapable of any resolute action. Pure, noble and sublime ideas can emanate only from a strong and healthy body. All religions are agreed on this point. Although the body is impermanent, special care should be taken to maintain it properly because it provides residence for the eternal Atma. The divine spirit illumines the body although the latter is composed of flesh, blood, faeces, urine and other foul-smelling and impure things. Atma does not grow with

24

the body, nor does it decay along with the body. The Atma principle is not subject to growth or decay. It is ever pure, precious and immutable.

Even if a big and brilliant diamond is found in a garbage heap, it does not lose its lustre or value. Just because a good variety of pumpkin is grown in a throny fence, there will be no change in its taste or cooking quality. Even though the peahen's egg is hatched under the warmth of the ordinary hen or fowl, the young peacock that emerges will not lose its beautiful plumage. So also, the splendour and effulgence of the selfless, stainless, eternal Atmic Principle will in no way be diminished although it is associated with the human body which is full of impurities.

What is the reason for people professing different faiths being agreed on the need to nourish the health and happiness of the body? It is because all of them regard the body as the temple of the Lord within. Therefore it is man's primary duty not to neglect this holy temple called the body, but to take utmost care for its proper maintenance and for using it for the discharge of one's duties and obligations in life. Persons who do not recognise this truth, subject the body to various ordeals in the name of worship, religious vows, fasting and penance. Thereby they are missing the goal of recognising the eternal Atmic Principle. By hitting the anthill, can you kill the snake inside it? By subjecting the body to torture, can you realise the Atma? By giving up good food and water, can you attain liberation? Self-realisation is possible only through knowing your own real nature.

Therefore, the first step in the quest for Self-knowledge is to understand the nature of man. Whatever the number of lives one might have had, the body he has now assumed is new. This shows that Divinity is inherent in man. The discovery of this Divinity or real Self of man calls for appropriate enquiry leading to the perception of the Real. When one perceives his real Self through prolonged contemplation on the Self, he becomes a Drashta (Seer). The ultimate aim of Bhakti-Devotion is to become such a Drashta and to experience the world with this spiritual perspective or background. Without this attainment, man remains a human being in form only, with no realisation of his true Self. The Sanskrit word "Manava" used to designate man, means "Not new", because his reality is the Atma which is ancient and eternal. Another meaning of the word "Manava" is: "Ma"-ajnana-ignorance; "na'- without; "va"- conducting oneself. In other words, he alone deserves the name of Manava (Man) who conducts himself without ignorance. Can all green birds speak like a parrot? Can every insect found on a flower be called a bee? Can a donkey become a tiger by merely putting on the skin of a tiger? Just because a pig has grown huge like an elephant, can it be called an elephant? Likewise can every one that has the human form be considered a real man? He alone can be rightly called a man, who has harmonised his thoughts, words and deeds.

The body is like a water bubble, which emerges from water, stays on water for a while, and merges back in water. So also the bubble called "Nara" (man) has emerged from the water called "Narayana" (God) and merges back in Him. Only when we recognise this Divine origin of the human being, will we take care to maintain and use the human body in an appropriate manner. Although the body is a mere instrument, its use has to be regulated according to prescribed standards and limits. Every object in the world is governed by certain regulations. It has rightly been said that we cannot achieve any success or progress without observing such discipline. The body too is governed by certain regulations. We should develop purity in our thoughts, feelings, looks, and actions. If on the other hand, one uses his senses and limbs in impure ways, one's nature would degenerate from human to demoniac. Our life can be compared to a business enterprise. The body's normal temperature is 98° F, if the temperature goes up to even 99°F , it is a symptom of disease. Our blood pressure too is 120/80mm, if it becomes more or less it is considered as disease. Even our eye ball can see light only within a particular range. Any deviation from the range will result in damage to the retina. Similarly our ears can hear sound within a given range; beyond that limit, the ear-drums will be damaged. Thus our body may be called a limited company. Hence we should observe these limits while making use of the body. Whether in the food we eat, or water we drink, or the words we speak and hear, in fact in all our living habits, moderation should be observed as the key-note. Exceeding the limits will entail danger. Excessive eating or talking results in mental aberration, while moderate eating or talking is conducive to pleasantness in life. Therefore the body should always be used in such a manner only, which confers happiness on man's life.

Man's knowledge can be classified into five categories. The type of knowledge which is most widely prevalent now-a-days is book knowledge. We are wasting our entire lives for acquiring such book knowledge which is merely superficial. On account of this, general knowledge and common sense have become conspicuous by their absence. These two, namely, general knowledge and common sense cannot be gained from books, but only

27

from various experiences in actual day-to-day living, especially through service to society. The fourth one is discriminative knowledge. This type of knowledge is now-a-days being used perversely for selfish ends. This is not the right use of discrimination. What is wanted is the kind of discrimination which keeps in view not the selfish individual good but the collective good of the society at large. Young people should particularly avoid justifying the wrong use of their discrimination for self-interest. They should develop what may be called "fundamental discrimination", which is equally applicable to all people, irrespective of the country to which they belong. Unlike in the case of ordinary arithmetic, 3-1=1 according to the spiritual arithmetic. You may argue that this equation is incorrect, but I firmly assert that it is correct. Why? Because it is based not on selfish wordly calculation but on selfless Atmic calculation which aims at universal welfare. Of the three entities God, Maya and the Universe, God is the object, Maya is the mirror and the Universe is God's reflection. If the mirror be removed, there will be no Maya and Universe. Then only God remains. Therefore, 3-1=1. People are not in a position to understand such things, because they lack the fifth type of knowledge viz., practical knowledge. This practical knowledge is highly essential for man, but it is woefully lacking to-day, because every individual thinks that it is enough to take care of himself only. He should realise that he is a part of society and that he should be equally concerned about the welfare of the society as a whole. There is no difference at all between the sun and his rays, or between the sea and its waves. Likewise there is no difference whatsoever between God and Love, because God is the source of Love. Similar is the relationship between the body and the

Atma which are interdependent and intimately associated with each other.

Although the body is transient, it should be properly cared for, till Atma is realised. Not recognising this truth, many persons neglect the body and expose themselves to the onslaught of many diseases. Even for achieving the four Purusharthas - goals of human life viz., Dharma, Artha, Kama, and Moksha bodily health is highly essential. Man to-day is subject to more maladies caused by mental worries than by consuming bad food. What is the shape of worry? It is only a mentally created fear. There should be a limit to speculation, anxiety and worries. Otherwise they will lead to mental troubles and derangement. A study of university students showed that 80 to 90 percent of the students in several universities were suffering from one or the other kind of mental disorders. Students should see that in this most precious stage of their lives, they do not become a prey to physical or mental ill-health. They should keep their minds away from unnecessary thoughts and worries, and also avoid excessive reading, playing, singing and sleeping etc., because excessive indulgence in any of such activities will have an adverse effect on the body.

Moreover, you have been told, off and on, about the programme of "Ceiling on Desires", which has four important components. The first one is: "Don't waste food". Why? Because food is God. Food is indispensable for human life, since the body cannot survive without food. The second one is: "Don't waste money". The misuse of money is an evil. To-day's youth especially are wasting money in a number of ways. This will lead to bad habits, loss of peace of mind and to the ruining of your life itself. Our country is to-day facing grave economic problems and therefore indiscriminate spending of money for selfish purposes should strictly be eschewed in the interest of the society at large. The spirit of co-operation has to be promoted. National unity and integrity should be safeguarded.

A balance has to be maintained between individual interests and national interests. Everything in life depends on maintaining the proper balance, whether it be walking, sitting, cycling or driving a car. To-day this balance has been lost because of excessive knowledge and its misuse. If knowledge is to be put to right use, it should be transformed into skill. However instead of skill, young people in particular, are killing knowledge. You are wasting knowledge and energy in seeing, hearing, talking, thinking etc., in wrong manner and in excessive measure. Therefore the third item in the "Ceiling on Desires", says, "Don't waste energy". A small illustration in this connection: you have tuned the radio to a particular station. Whether the volume is kept high or low, whether you listen or not, so many units of electrical energy will be wasted. Likewise your body is a radio. You are constantly engaged in thinking as well as talking in a loud or low tone, talking to others or to yourself, talking while awake and even while asleep. Due to such continuous talking day and night, how much of energy is being wasted, thereby causing allergy in your lives. Every action involves the use of energy. If the energy in the body is properly utilised, then balance will be maintained and the body will be in good shape.

The fourth dictum of the "Ceiling on Desires" is "Don't waste time". Students, only when the body is strong, healthy and happy can you enjoy the proper state of balance in life. Man's life is wasted in brooding over the past and worrying about the future. What is the root cause of man's sorrow and sickness? Not being content with what he has, and hankering after what he does not have, man forfeits peace of mind. There is no need to think about what is past or about what is in store in the future. Of what avail is it to think of the past which is irrevocable or to worry about the future which is uncertain? It is a sheer waste of time. Past is past, future is future. You can do nothing about either. What is most important is the present. This is not ordinary present. It is Omnipresent. The result of the past and the result of the future are both present in the present. You are reaping in the present what you had sown in the past. And what you are sowing in the present, you will reap in future. Thus both the past and the future are contained in the present only. So, make the best use of the present. Give up all sorts of worry and lead ideal lives leading to immortality and fulfilment of the purpose of human life.

Students, don't underestimate the value of the body. Everything in this world is impermanent; on that account, are we neglecting such things? So, even though the body is trasient, you should take good care of it so long as it lasts, because it is a moving temple of God. Develop self-confidence instead of confidence in the world. Self-confidence may be compared to the foundation for the edifice of life, self-satisfaction is like the walls, self-sacrifice is the roof and Self-realisation is the happiness of living in the mansion of human body. Therefore with self-confidence, you can accomplish anything and secure joy. You will be able to face and surmount any difficulties in life.

What do you mean by Self? Self is of two kinds. One is the single lettered 'I' . The other is the three-lettered 'eye', which stands for the body. The single-lettered 'I' refers to the Atma which is present in all. There may be some people who may not have the three-lettered 'eye' or even if it is there, it may be covered by cataract or suffer from other defects or diseases. But the single lettered 'I' exists equally in all persons irrespective of whether one is a Bhogi (hedonist or pleasure-seeker), Rogi (diseased person), Yogi (realised person), Viragi (the renunciate or monk) or Byragi (mendicant).

Whenever a number of people are called severally by their names, each of them will respond saying 'I'. Although their names and forms are different, the 'I' in all of them is one and the same. That is why the Vedas have declared, *"Ekam Sat vipra bahudha vadanti"*, which means "Truth (or Existence) is one; but the sages call it by various names". You should therefore, try to experience the unity underlying the diversity in the universe. It is because you see the diversity ignoring the unity, there is so much restlessness and lack of peace in the world. For instance, nations are many but earth is one; stars are many but sky is one, beings are many, but breath is one. Therefore, if man remembers this unity in diversity, there will be no room for differences, quarrels or wars in the world.

Students, you are now in the most precious period of your life. You should never give room for any differences and discrimination in your thoughts, words or deeds. Such unhealthy ideas arise from an unhealthy body. Each of you can judge for yourself whether you are strong and healthy or weak and unhealthy, based on the nature of ideas that arise in you. That is why it is said *"Yat bhavam tat bhavati"*, i.e., "As you think, so you become". Just as you take care of the iron safe for the sake of the valuable jewels inside, so too you should take care of your body for the sake of the precious Atma in it. You should eat to live but not live to eat. If you have self-confidence, the required food will come walking to you, as it were. You need not go in search of food. That is why it is said in the Bhagavat that one who seeks the Atma is a Gopi (Devotee) while one who seeks food is a Papi (Sinner). It is a pity that having got the invaluable human birth, people are running after Anna (food) instead of seeking the Atma. Vedanta has been exhorting man to find out who he really is. Instead of using the mirror of your intellect for looking at your self, you are placing the mirror in front of others to see them. That is why you are not able to see yourself.

Develop self-confidence which will lead you to bliss. Never give room for worries and anxieties. Gain sufficient strength of the body and mind to face boldly the difficulties, losses and sorrows that may confront you in life. This will be facilitated, if you practise the four F's taught in our educational system viz., "Follow the Master (your conscience)", "Face the Devil", "Fight till the end", and "Finish the game". What is the inner meaning of the first three alphabets A,B,C in the English language? It means Always Be Careful. The same dictum is given by the Upanishad by exhorting a man to "arise, awake and stop not till the goal is reached".

However long you may live, whatever scientific knowledge you may acquire, whatever position you may occupy, some time or other you have to know the Truth about yourself. Start knowing it from now itself. You should be on the alert all the time, because you can never know when the Lord's Grace, His Love and Benediction will be showered on you, at what time and at what place and in what circumstances. Unlike in the case of wordly

33

matters, you cannot understand what is happening in the spiritual domain or what the Divine plans are. Therefore, if you go on discharging your duties and obligations in the proper manner with enthusiasm and joy, that itself will confer bliss on you. Don't worry about the future. Don't brood over the past. All are passing clouds only. In this world, there is nothing permanent, whether persons, objects or other things. The very name Jagat (Universe) means "coming and going". Knowing this truth, why should you worry at all? So give no scope whatsoever for any kind of worry. Only then can man be entitled to become divine.

It is only man that is endowed with the capacity to discover his Divinity. In this context, food habits play an important role. Out of 84,00,000 species of living beings on earth, 83,99,999 species of creatures like insects, birds, animals and beasts etc., live on what is provided by God in Nature, and hence they do not generally suffer from any diseases. Man is the sole exception in this regard. By becoming a slave to his palate, he relishes only cooked and spicy foods of various kinds, without realising to what extent such foods are curtailing his own longevity.

Besides this, it is significant to note that those who live on vegetarian food are less prone to diseases whereas non-vegetarians are subject to more diseases. Why? Because animal food is incompatible with the needs of the human body. Doctors speak about proteins being present in non-vegetarian food, but the fact is that there are better quality proteins in food articles like vegetables, pulses, milk, curd, etc. Non-vegetarian food not only affects man's body but also has deleterious effect on his mind.

Food, Head, God - these three are inter-related. By consuming animal food, animal tendencies are aroused. As is your food, so are your thoughts. Men to-day are behaving in a manner worse than that of wild animals in the forest. They have become cruel, pitiless and hard-hearted. There is no sympathy or understanding even between man and man. The main reason for this condition lies in the kind of food that is consumed. Students, be careful about the food you eat. See that it is conducive to your health and happiness. Our ancestors used to take food twice a day and our ancient sages used to eat only once a day They declared that the man who eats only once is a Yogi, the one who eats twice a day is a Bhogi (enjoyer) and he who eats thrice a day is a Rogi (sick man). Today people go on consuming food at all times, not to speak of drinks and snacks in between. How then can they escape from indigestion and other diseases? Man needs food which supplies him energy equivalent to about one calorie per minute. Young people should be satisfied with 2000 calories of food per day. For healthy life, man needs only 1,500 calories per day. But now-a-days the food intake has increased upto 5000 calories. As a result, people suffer from indigestion and sleeplessness. Loss of sleep gives rise to may ailments. Don't worry about sleep. If you go to bed without any worry, you will get sound sleep automatically.

Observe moderation in your intake of food as well as in other living habits, to keep your body in good shape and to perform your duties properly. However, do not develop undue attachment to the body. The two feelings of 'I' and 'Mine' are solely responsible for all the problems and evils prevailing in society. You should try to minimise, if not eliminate altogether the feelings of "doership" and enjoyership". Then only you will be able to lead ideal lives.

We sufer from ill-health due to psychological reasons also. If you examine your pulse, blood pressure, temperature etc.,, with feeling or fear that you are unwell, you will get abnormal readings. If you have the apprehension that you will not get good sleep, it will happen accordingly. So always try to have a positive outlook and self-confidence that your health is alright. Our ancients wished to live long for the sake of a Godly life and therefore tried to preserve the health of their bodies as well as minds accordingly. To-day one is called on old man, if he attains the age of sixty or seventy. But in olden days, people were considered young even at the age of 80,90 or 100. Students, you might have read in the Mahabharata that at the time of the Kurukshetra war, Krishna and Arjuna were 86 years, and 84 years old respectively. But they were in youthful condition and participated in the war with vigour, vitality and valour. Who was the Commander-in-chief of the Kaurava army? It was the 116 year old Bhishma. If it were to be to-day, a 116 year old man would be confined to his cot, with his body shaking all over and needing others' help even for getting up from bed. But Bhishma fought fiercely for nine days. How do you account for this? It was because of their mental strength, nourshing food, and above all Self-confidence (confidence in the real Self, Atma). To-day such spiritual strength is totally lacking among the people. Self-confidence is constantly going up and down. Their minds are unsteady and subject to jumps and bumps from moment to moment. If their wishes are fulfilled, they will instal ten pictures of God instead of one in their shrine room. In case their desires are not complied with, they will remove even the one picture which they used to worship previously. This is an indication of the way -wardness of their mind, This is not the right attitude.

You may worship a picture as God but not God as a picture. If your mind wavers from moment to moment, how can there be steadiness or stability in life? Every one must endeavour to develop the courage to face the vicissitudes of life, joys or sorrows, gains or losses, with equanimity.

To-day there are many who profess themselves to be believers in God. But because these so-called believers do not conduct themselves properly, many are becoming atheists. Talking about Bhakti (devotion), they resort to Bhukti (hedonism). This is no genuine devotion. A devotee should be ready to gladly accept anything as God's gift. Can you get sugar by merely requesting the sugar cane, instead of crushing it to extract the juice from it? Even if it be the best kind of diamond, will it shine in all its effulgence, unless it is subjected to cutting and polishing? Similarly, it is only when man undergoes trials and tribulations, hardships, losses and sorrows that his real worth will shine forth. Bhakti (devotion) is the nectar obtained as a result of churning the essences of many Upanishads and Scriptures. Real devotion is that which is buttressed by firm faith and is steadfast and unchanging under all circumstances. Only then does one deserve to get the fruits of real Bhakti-devotion.

Embodiments of Divine Love! Although you may have body-consciousness, your lives should be guided by the Atmic awareness. The body, the senses, the mind, the intellect and the Atma are to be considered as your five-breaths (Pancha Pranas). Once you have understood the mysteries or subtleties of each of them you need no other spiriutal discipline. Truth is everything. Without realising this, what is the use of troubling yourselves with all sorts of Sadhanas- spiritual practices? I am explaining to you, during this summer course, about the subtle truths relating to the five vital constituents of your personality in compliance with the request of your Vice-Chancellor. You speak about meditation. What do you do in meditation? You are merely sitting in a comfortable posture, with your eyes closed. But your mind is wandering in the barber's shop, or washerman's laundry or in the bazaar (market place). Instead of engaging yourself in such futile exercises, you had better enter into the Society and undertake selfless service. Without understanding what real meditation is, your attempts at meditation will result only in sound sleep. First of all try to understand the nature of the mind. Then only will you be able to control it. Once an old woman came to me and complained that her mind was giving her endless trouble by its restless wanderings. Then I asked her, "Where is that mind which is troubling you? Show it to me and I shall destroy it". She replied "Swami, I don't know where it is". I told her, "If you do not know where the mind is, how do you say it is troubling you? Is it the mind that is troubling you or are you troubling yourself" So without understanding anything about the mind, to blame it, is meaningless and to sit in meditation is sheer idleness. You must, therefore, have a thorough understanding of the nature of the mind as well as the senses. Everything in the world has some useful secrets to reveal. God does not create anything without a purpose. All things are purposeful, meaningful, blissful and valuable. But we are not making any effort to understand their mysteries. Hence I hope and bless that during this fortnight you will understand thoroughly the nature and the role of the body, the senses, the mind, the intellect and the Atma, so that you may blossom forth as ideal students endowed with purity and equanimity.

───────────── ❧ ─────────────

Mastery of the Senses

One may acquire great scholarship and
come out victorious in assemblies of scholars;
One may be a great hero and win battles galore;
One may be born as a king of kings and rule a
vast empire;
One may generously give away in charity gold and cows;
One may be able to count the countless
stars that adorn the sky;
One may be able to name the innumerable
species of living beings;
One may be well-versed in Ashtanga
Vidya (the eight-fold path of Yoga);
One may be successful in reaching the Moon;
But no one can control his body and senses,
Nor conquer his mind and keep it
In a state of constant introversion and
unshakeable equanimity.

It is true that the body wields some influence over the senses. But the senses have even greater influence on the body. There can be no body without the senses nor senses without the body. These two are inseparable and interdependent. Negative without positive, or positive without negative (in the case of electric current) will serve no purpose. Likewise, a body without senses, or senses without a body cannot function. Hence it is imperative for every person to take proper care of the body.

The role of the senses is remarkable. The wonders performed by the Divine defy description. But the part played by the senses is even more marvellous and mysterious. Strange, unpredictable and indescribable indeed are the ways of the sense organs. The senses are subtler than the body. Although the faculties of speech,

39

touch, sight, hearing and taste as well as gas, bile and phlegm exist in the body, the senses exercise extraordinary control over all of them equally. Joy and sorrow, heat and cold etc., are experienced only when the sense organs come in contact with external objects. Without the sensory objects, the senses cannot function even for a moment. All the activities of the senses are oriented towards the objects in the environment. It is not possible for us to comprehend or describe the myriad facets of sense organs and their activities.

The senses are also called by the name "Maatraah", which means "measuring instruments". How is this measuring done by the sense organs? Take a fruit, for instance. Which of the senses has the capacity to determine whether it is sweet or sour? Which is the sense organ that measures or decides the taste of an object? It is the tongue. The tongue determines the taste of an eatable, decides whether it is good or bad and makes it known to all concerned.

Which organ is capable of declaring whether a picture is attractive or ugly? The eye alone is the measuring rod for this purpose. Similarly, the power to determine whether an object is fragrant or foul-smelling is vested in the nose. Likewise it is the ear that can discriminate between a melodious musical note and a discordant one. Thus, the sense organs are called "Maatraah" in as much as they are endowed with the capacity to measure and determine the particular quality or characteristic of different sense objects.

In the Kathopanishad, the senses are described as horses yoked to the chariot of the body. What is the inner significance of naming the senses as horses (Aswa in Sanskrit)? "Aswa" means that which is always restless. It is common knowledge that a horse, whether it is standing or running or even sleeping, moves some part of its body or the other all the time, whether the tail, or the leg, or the back or the nose, or the jaws. It is because of this restless nature of the horse that it is called "Aswam". Similarly, take the case of the peepul tree (*Ficus religiosa*). Whether there is any breeze or not, its leaves are constantly rustling, Hence it is called "Aswattha" tree.

In ancient times, the Indian rulers used to perform a sacrifice (Yaga) by name "Aswa-Medha Yaga". "Aswa" means fickle. "Medha" means 'Buddhi (intellect)'. Thus "Aswa - Medha" means 'Fickle-minded'. Hence the horse that is used in the sacrifice symbolises a fickle mind. Whosoever is capable of capturing and controlling that horse is described as "Dheemantha" (a man of heroic intelligence), worthy of combat. Here we see the esoteric and exoteric meanings of the term "Aswa-Medha". It is only when both the meanings are taken together that we get at the whole truth. To-day it is the duty of every person to control the horse-like senses. Only then can he be called a hero in the true sense. Whatever Yagas, Yajnas or other rituals one may perform, whatever Scriptures he might have mastered, if he has no control over his senses, all these accomplishments are worthless.

The term "Maatraah" as applied to the senses has yet another meaning. It indicates that the limit to what can be experienced by each sense organ, has been prescribed by the Lord Divine. For instance, the eye can only see, but cannot hear. The mouth can only speak, but cannot see. Thus each organ has been endowed by God with a specific talent only. Those who use these organs according to the divinely-prescribed functions will alone be acting up to the will of the Divine. Those who violate the prescribed limits will be transgressing the Divine will, thereby becoming liable for punishment.

41

Everyone, therefore, should make use of the sense organs with due regard to the functions and limits prescribed for each of them. For example, the nose has been allotted a specific assignment of inhaling and exhaling air for preserving one's health, and of distinguishing between good and bad smells, and take in only what is good and fragrant. Ignoring this specific role ordained for the nose, to-day's man unfortunately is misusing it for taking snuff and inhalaing foul odours. By such practices, he is violating the injunctions pertaining to the use of the nose. Thereby he commits a double offence; one, violating a Divine injuction and the other, causing damage to his health. No wonder, therefore, that man to-day has become a prey to all kinds of disease.

In the same manner, the tongue has been given to man to consume wholesome food which promotes his health as well as to speak gently and sweetly so as to give joy to others, and to communicate his inner-most thoughts and feelings to others. The tongue, which has been bestowed on us for such edifying purposes, is being grossly misused now-a-days. It is being used for consuming drugs and narcotics, eating animal food, smoking, indulging in abuse of others, carrying tales, back-biting, and speaking harsh words that hurt others, etc. Through such perverse use of the tongue, the Divine injuctions are violated by setting at naught the ordained limits. Consequently, man has to experience numerous troubles.

It is only by properly using the God-given senses for the purposes for which they are intended that man can rise to Divine heights. Just because you have the sense organs, you should not use them as you please. They are like horses yoked to a chariot. You must know how to handle them properly so that the chariot can run smoothly and safely along the right road to the ultimate goal of life. The horses must be in front of the chariot. To-day on the contrary, the horses are placed behind the chariot. This is leading to dangerous consequences. If, on the plea that the senses should be respected and given a place of honour, you place the horses (senses) inside the chariot, how can the chariot move at all? While fostering the senses, no effort is being made to bring them under control internally. This amounts to feeding a horse excessively and unduly fattening it, but not giving it adequate work. This is sure to have untoward results. To-day we are pampering the senses but not giving them any work. That is why they are running amuck, spelling disaster to the master himself. The senses should be put to right use as ordained by God; otherwise, man will have to suffer from lack of peace.

This situation may be compared to that of a man with many wives. King Uttanapaada had two wives and because of the differences between them, the child Dhruva had to go to the forest to perform penance. King Dasaratha had three wives. To comply with the demands of his youngest wife, he had to endure the exile of his dearest son, Rama, to the forest, eventually to lose his life due to the pangs of separation. If this be the plight of those having two or three wives, imagine the condition of one who has to manage ten wives! For, this V.I.P (very important person), namely the mind, has to manage ten wives - the five sense organs and the five organs of action. Each organ insists on enjoying objects of its own choice. For example, the nose is attracted by the smell of "Masala Dosa" (a South Indian dilicacy) and wants to have it. The ear wants the radio to be tuned, so that it can enjoy melodious music. The eyes hanker after a new film. Thus when all of them are keen about their own particular desires, how can the master (the mind) satisfy them all

43

at the same time? Unable to satisfy them, the mind gets frustrated. How then can this mind wedded to ten wives enjoy peace? It is only when the senses are kept under proper control that man can be happy himself and share that happiness with those around him.

There is a method by which the demands of the senses can be reconciled and harmonised. This is by treating both good and bad with equal-mindedness. Tukaram is an illustrious example in this regard. He was a great devotee and very gentle by nature. His wife was a shrew. Nevertheless, by his calmness and forbearance, Tukaram managed to get on well with her. Only when one is in the habit of retaliating word for word, tit for tat, tooth for tooth and nail for nail, one has to face discord and trouble. But Tukaram was the very embodiment of forbearance. He used to cultivate his small farm of half-an-acre to maintain his family. At the instance of his neighbours, he once raised sugarcane crop in that small plot of land. When the crop was mature taking undue advantage of Tukaram's good nature, many passers-by used to pluck a couple of sugarcanes and chew them. Finally, Tukaram harvested whatever crop was left behind, bundled the canes and was taking them home in his cart. On the way, the children of the village gathered round him and pleaded for a piece of sugarcane each. In his usual generosity, Tukaram allowed the children to help themselves to the canes in the cart. At last when he reached home, there was only one cane left in the cart. Seeing this, his wife flew into a rage and strongly scolded Tukaram, condemning him as unfit for family life; she took out the only cane on the cart in a fit of anger and struck Tukaram with it. The cane broke into three pieces, out of which two fell on the ground, and the other was in her hand. Tukaram calmly remarked, "I was wondering all along the way as to how to distribute the single remaining cane to the three members of the family. I am glad you have nicely solved the problem for me. You can eat one piece which is in your hand, and give the other two which have fallen on the floor to the two children". Such forbearance and equanimity can rarely be found except in a few high-souled persons. These qualities can be acquired only through devotion and faith. You need not feel disheartened with the fear that you will not be able to control the senses. By developing one-pointed devotion and complete surrender to God, the senses can definitely be brought under control.

Kabir is an example of another godly man in a different situation. Unlike Tukaram's wife, Kabir's wife was highly devoted and faithful, totally dedicated to serving the husband and obeying him implicitly. One day Kabir was plying his handloom, chanting as usual, the name of "Ram" all the time. Suddenly he called his wife and saying that one thread has snapped, he asked her to bring a lamp. It was noon and when she brought the lightened lamp, Kabir asked her to take it back as it was not necessary (because of daylight). Any other wife in her position would have retorted, saying, "Have you no eyes to see the daylight? Why did you waste my time and effort by unnecessarily asking me to bring a lighted lamp and to take it back? Do you think I have no other work?" etc. But Kabir's wife was made of a different stuff. She silently took back the lamp, without a murmur or uttering even a single word of resentment. Hence, with such a dutiful and obedient wife, Kabir was able to develop his devotion unhampered, and expressed his gratitude to God for His Grace in giving him such a good partner in life.

Here you have two examples of saintly men, who, despite their contrasting family situations, pursued their spiritual path equally well. Hence it is not the environment that matters in the control of one's senses and emotions. It is the purity of one's impulses, sincerity of purpose and determination in treading the divine path which count rather than the environment which is of little or no consequence in this regard.

You must have heard about Einstein who was a great scientist as well as a man of wisdom - a rare combination. He had a very stupid woman. She was not only uneducated but also rude in her behaviour. Einstein was always engaged in experiments, investigations, and also contemplation. He was so much absorbed in his work that he never used to go in time for his food and refreshments, even though frequently reminded by his wife. His wife was upset and disgusted with the behaviour of her husband and used to lose her temper quite often. One day, she was feeling very hungry. She served all the dishes on the dinner table and repeatedly requested her husband to come and have his food. But Einstein paid no heed to her words, as he was engrossed with his thoughts forgetful of the world outside. His wife became enraged at this and rushed to him with a jugful of water and emptied it on her husband's head along with a shower of rebukes. Einstein was not upset, though fully drenched. He smiled at his wife and cooly remarked, "Everyday, it used to be only lightning and thunder. But to-day it is a heavy down-pour on my head"! Just imagine the forbearance, composure and humour of Einstein in such a highly trying and provoking situation! If it were to be any other husband, he would have smashed the wife's head with the very same empty jug snatching it from her hand. But Einstein never thought in terms of such retaliation or even retort for that matter. Such was his control over his senses!

The ancient sages regarded sense-control as a form of penance. To discipline the senses, one should understand how the senses function. Here is a small story to illustrate how a christian priest learnt a lesson in sense control from the driver of a horse carriage in which he was travelling. The priest noticed that the driver was beating the horse severely as it was approaching a railway crossing. The priest who was a strong believer in Christ's message of love and compassion, took pity on the animal, and asked the driver why he was beating the horse unnecessarily, although it was running alright. The driver explained that at the level crossing there were some white painted stones which created a fright in the horse. He was beating the animal as it was more afraid of the whip than the white stones, and would therefore, proceed through the level crossing, without halting due to the fear of the white stones. So the priest learnt the lesson that when the attention of any sense organ is distracted by something, it should be diverted to another desirable thing by means of a stronger incentive or disincentive. Then only will it give up its crazy digressions and take to the right path.

Suppose there is an animal which has developed the bad habit of stealthily grazing the crops in others' fields. How to wean it away from the bad habit? If you feed that animal in your cattle-stall with green fodder which is even more palatable than the field crops, it will get used to stall-feeding, and will thereby give up its bad habit of grazing field crops. Likewise, the senses should be weaned away from their bad habits and trained properly to take to good habits.

The senses have been compared to "Pasu" (animals). The word "Pasu" means the one whose vision is externally oriented. The one having an inner vision is called "Pasupati"

47

or "the Lord of animals" (Siva). Man should aspire and strive to become a "Pasupati" or master of the senses, but not a "Pasu", a slave of the senses. It is a pity that to-day's man has become a slave of the senses. There are several ways of taming the senses and putting them on the proper path. In this connection, it is important to avoid pampering the senses.

If you investigate carefully about the birth place of the sense-pleasures, you will find that they have their origin in sorrow only. That is why every sense pleasure carries with it the sting of sorrow. The pleasure derived from the senses is momentary and ultimately ends up in grief only. Desires arise this moment and subside the next moment. Suppose the desire to eat Laddu (sweet) arises in you to-day. No sooner have you eaten two Laddus than you develop satiation or aversion for the sweet. Desire this moment and disgust next moment! Pleasure and pain in quick succession! By thus contemplating on the momentary and deceptive nature of the so-called sense-pleasures, we can develop discrimination and detachment and keep the senses under check. Another important point you should note is that, if the senses are kept busy in the right way, there will be no trouble from them. Otherwise, you will become their slave.

Eventhough I may not be physically present, I know what is going on at a particular place at a particular time as well as the inner feelings of the people concerned. For instance, this afternoon, Dr. Hemalatha, Principal of the Women's College, Anantpur, entertained all of you with a very illuminating lecture on Prahlada, interspersed with melodious songs and poems in Telugu. One of the most important things she mentioned was how Hiranyakashipu who hated and abused Hari (Lord Vishnu)

48

was killed by the latter and was redeemed thereby. Similarly in the case of Lord Krishna, he was being always abused strongly by people like Sisupala and Dantavakra. Once in the great assembly hall of Dharmaja (Yudhistira) packed with a distinguished gathering of eminent people, the question arose as to who should be given the first offering (or primacy) of respect and honour, i.e., "Agra Thamboolam", (literally meaning, the first offering of pan supari or betel leaves and arecanut). Although there were several men of distinction like Bhishma, Drona, etc., the Pandavas decided to give this unique honour only to Sri Krishna who was their all in all, who stood by them through thick and thin and who came to their rescue during many a crisis. Dharmaja washed Krishna's feet and gave him the first offering of respect and honour. Wicked persons cannot understand the inner meaning and motives of other people. Guided merely by external formalities and selfish considerations, they criticise and abuse others out of malice and envy. This was exactly what the narrow-minded Sisupala did on that occasion. He could not tolerate Krishna being honoured thus in that great assembly of eminent personages. Right in front of the great teachers, great sages and great men of honour and distinction, the wicked Sisupala began showering virulent abuses on Sri Krishna, mentioning for instance that Krishna was a thief who stole butter from others' houses, and who robbed the innocent cow-herd girls of their sarees, out-raging their modesty and indulging in fun and frolic with them and that therefore it was a wanton affront to the august assembly to give the primacy of honour to Krishna. When this type of vituperative abuse by Sisupala exceeded the limits, Krishna suddenly threw at Sisupala the very plate in which Dharmaja made his offering to Krishna. Some say that Krishna threw His Sudarshan.

Chakra at Sisupala. But that is not correct. It was only with the throwing of the plate that Krishna severed Sisupala's head. Dharmaja was exceedingly happy that the wicked Sisupala was slain by Krishna. But the very next moment, his happiness turned into utter surprise and bewilderment, as if his mind was struck by a severe cyclone, when he witnessed the blood from the severed neck of Sisupala falling on Krishna's sacred feet, and what was more surprising when the life-flame emerging from Sisupala's body merged in Sri Krishna. Amazed at his strange phenomenon, Dharmaja questioned Narada how such a traitor and vicious enemy of Krishna like Sisupala could have such a glorious end, by way of the merger of his spirit in Sri Krishna - a consummation which even devotees who have surrendered themselves to the Divine can hardly expect. To this Narada replied, "Abuse or praise, vilification or veneration pertain to the body only and not to the Atma which is beyond all pairs of opposites. The one Supreme Paramatma alone dwells in all beings. That being the case, who is the reviler and who the reviled? Who is a friend and who a foe? All are the same. The blood that is saturated with the constant remembrance of God becomes an offering dedicated to God. Whether out of hatred or love, lust or envy, ego or surrender, whatever be the feelings, it is enough if the Lord's name is remembered incessantly". Sisupala remembered Sri Krishna's name more often than many devotees. Devotees remember God only when they see the temples and their towers or pictures and idols installed therein. But Sisupala, out of his intense hatred for Krishna, had Krishna in his mind in all places and at all times whether waking or sleeping. It was because of this ceaseless remembrance of Sri Krishna that Sisupala's soul could merge in Him.

Worldly persons look only at the superficial and external aspects of things and actions. But the Lord does not see things that way. He is free from hatred or envy, likes or dislikes. When these are attributed to the Lord, they are but a reflection of your own feelings. God is like a clean mirror. What you see therein is but a mere reflection of your own actions and postures - grin for a grin, smile for a smile, salute for a salute and so on. For God, there is no action or reaction. God neither punishes nor rewards any one. You are punished or rewarded by your own actions. Hence no one is entitled to question the actions of God, accusing God of favouritism to some, and indifference to some others. Who has the authority to dictate to God how He should conduct Himself? The Divinity present in every one may find expression in various types of behaviour. But the actions of the Divine are always full of love and entirely free from selfishness and therefore totally taintless. That is why God has several appelations like "attributeless, taintless, ancient, the abode for all, eternal, pure, enlightened (consciousness), free", etc. God's eye does not see purity or impurity. It is all in your vision only. As you think, so you become. You look at the world through coloured glasses and wrongly attributed those colours to the world. It is your defective vision that makes you see defects which do not exist in creation.

The defects which you attribute to the senses are, in fact, the defects in your own thought processes and feelings. If the senses are properly used, they will offer you the right impressions. For example, Tukaram had good feelings and so gave a favourable interpretation to even the rude and negative behaviour of his wife; his senses did not stand in the way of his spiritual progress and equanimity, despite trying circumstances in his family.

51

Likewise, Kabir was always engaged in remembrance of God and hence his wife's behaviour was harmonious and conducive to his spiritual advancement. Einstein, too, had the quality of equanimity in him and therefore he was not at all upset by the biosterous behaviour of his wife. From all these instances, it is evident that what you need to do is to harmonise your own thoughts and feelings through proper sadhana (spiritual discipline), rather than blame the environment or other persons for your shortcomings.

However, some stubbron people given to vain argumentation, blame God for giving an out-going orientation to man's senses. They argue that God has given them eyes with doors which open to the outside world; ears which can hear external sounds; and noses that can only inhale the air from outside. They contend, therefore, that the fault lies with the creator only and not with them. They try to justify their sensuous behaviour, by saying that, "to err is human". Such misleading rationalisation is a travesty of truth and is worthy of strong condemnation, especially when it is indulged in by the youth. If animals behave wrongly, it is quite understandable, because they are not endowed with the faculty of discrimination to control and guide their senses. But if man, who is blessed by God with the power of discrimination, takes to the wrong path, yielding to his senses, it is highly unparadonable. How paradoxical and ridiculous it is to be born as a man and to behave as an animal; behave, therefore, as befits a human being.

Some students who consider themselves to be very smart, try to argue thus: "Look at the birds, cattle and beasts. They are having full freedom to eat what they want, to mate as they like and to fly or wander as they wish.

Why should man be denied such freedom as is enjoyed by these lower animals?" A specious argument indeed! But let us ask these wiseacres, "what kind of freedom do the animals enjoy?" The answer undoubtedly is: "animal freedom". Animals enjoy animal freedom. There is nothing wrong in it. But being a man, is it not wrong and unbecoming of you to want to enjoy animal freedom? You try to give several wrong meanings and misleading interpretations to the word "freedom". What you should strive for is freedom from the senses and not freedom of the senses. True freedom is to control the senses and the lower self in an attempt to attain the higher (real) Self and experience the eternal bliss of the Atma (Atmananda).

Along with knowledge, it is important to have character also. Then only you can enjoy a perfect balance in life. It is a pity that to-day's education caters only to the development of intelligence and cleverness ignoring character and human values altogether. What is the use of acquiring any amount of knowledge available in the world, if one does not have character? This is the reason for the loss of balance in the case of the modern men in general and the educated men in particular. If you lose your balance while riding a bicycle, you are liable to meet with accidents. Similarly, if there is a lack of balance between knowledge and character in your life's journey you are surely exposing yourself to serious accidents. Therefore you have to control the senses on the one hand and develop virtuous living on the other. It is highly essential for students to maintain the balance between the two. Students! It will not do if you merely exercise control over your senses. You should also harmonise them. According to Patanjali, Yoga is the control of the wanderings of the mind. However, such control of the mind is most difficult, if not altogether impossible, to achieve.

The appropriate and easy method, on the contrary, is to achieve mental harmony or balance. Concentrate on what is good, and then you will be automatically keeping yourself away from what is bad. It is the weakness of your mind that is responsible for all your problems. There was a foreigner by name Carlyle. He was highly intelligent, but due to lack of control over his senses, he became very weak. He was suffering from insomnia. One day, he called his neighbour and complained to him that he was unable to sleep during night time, because of the crowing of the cock in that neighbour's house. The neighbour replied that no cock would crow throughout night, but only twice or thrice and that in spite of having the cock in his house, he (neighbour) was able to sleep well. Carlyle's reply to this was that he too knew that the cock crows only two or three times, but he was unable to sleep, because he was always thinking of the cock and its crowing at any time of the night. The lesson of the story is that Carlyle's loss of sleep was not due to the crowing of the cock as alleged by him, but only due to his own imaginary fear. Likewise most people now-a-days suffer not on account of their senses, but only due to all sorts of wrong imaginations. So man should completely give up such imaginations and baseless fears, which are detrimental to him. In the next few days, we shall consider some more aspects of the senses, their mastery and harmonisation.

Road to Divinity

In the worthless mens' hearts devoid of purity,
Do abide the vices of anger and envy.
Don't bats abound in dens of darkness?
Never should you forget this wise saying.

He alone is a man who seeks the One
Who blest his ears with the power to hear
And endowed his eyes with the glow of sight.

Embodiments of Divine Love!

Control of the senses must be the primary aim of the students, but not the fleeting pleasures of the sense objects, which give but a little momentary joy followed by endless misery. The sensory perceptions, namely, hearing, touching seeing, tasting and smelling are more powerful than the sense organs. The most important among the sense organs is the tongue. If the tongue is conquered, it virtually amounts to mastering all the senses. The tongue has two important functions: eating and talking. Whoever is able to conquer these two faculties of the tongue can merge himself in the Divine Self. When the tongue stops talking, the mind starts chatting. To control the mind's prattling, the intellect has to be awakened. Then one should gently persuade the intellect to turn gradually towards the Atma.

True Sadhana - Spiritual practice - consists in the technique of merging the Vaak - faculty of speech - in the mind, the mind in the intellect, and finally the intellect in the Atma. Forgetting this sacred and royal road available to man, it is sad that he chooses to indulge in sensual pleasures which ultimately drown him in deep sorrow. No one tries to find out what the ultimate source of animation for the insentient senses is, nor does one seeks to know who the real enjoyer is of all the pleasures derived through the senses. Students should recognise that there is an intimate relationship between the external world and the internal world within oneself. Is it the body or the senses or the Atma that experiences the pleasures of eating delicious food or seeing a beautiful sight, or smelling a fragrant object? It is not the body, much less the sense organs. The real experiencer in all these cases is the Atma which is the causeless cause of all that exists, and which fosters, sustains, presides and rules over all the things in the universe. Atma is the basis for the manifested world and the original source of motivation for the internal world. Only when we recognise the cardinal role of the Atma as the root cause of everything, the deceptive and transient sense organs will cease to have dominance over us.

Of all the sense organs, the tongue has an overriding importance and influence. Mastery over this one sense organ will enable one to master easily all the other sense organs. The Kathopanishad has compared the senses to horses. A horse can run fast; but once a bridle is put in its mouth and held tight, its entire movement can be easily controlled. How is it that a small bridle is able to control such a large, strong and fast-running animal? Because, the mouth is the most important and vulnerable part of the horse from the stand point of keeping it under control. Once the mouth is bridled, the entire animal comes under control. Likewise in the case of man also, the mouth is the most important among the five sense organs. With the help of a small rudder, we can save a big boat from a fierce cyclone. With a small spark we can kindle a bonfire. The power of speech is like a spark of fire. By controlling the tongue one can virtually acquire control over the world itself. The power of speech can be used either for a noble and sublime purpose or misused in a mean and mischievous manner. It can be utilised for blessing people or for blaming others. Bilwamangal - alias Jayadeva - sings thus addressing the tongue in words that combine compliments with counselling; "Oh my dear tongue! You are sweet. You have the capacity to discriminate between good and bad taste. So I am telling you the supremely benevolent truth: do not indulge in idle talk; instead of it make yourself busy by singing the sweet and glorious names of the Lord - Govinda!, Damodara!, Madhava!, etc." There is a familiar saying "A slip of the foot may not cause much harm, but a slip of the tongue will land you in hell". A reckless use of your tongue can grievously hurt others' hearts. And no doctor on earth can heal the wound caused by a harsh word.

When the senses come in contact with sense objects, they can give rise to immense pleasure as well as endless pain. For instance, someone outside is abusing you; so long as the abuse is beyond the range of your sense organs, you are not in any way affected by it. But once the abusive words reach your ears, you become enraged and excited beyond control. What is the reason for your being upset like that? As long as there was no contact between the sound waves and your ears, you were unruffled. It was the subsequent contact between the two that provoked the strong reaction in you. To take a contrasting example: some one outside is praising you, extolling your admirable qualities. So long as you have not heard his words of praise, you derive no joy nor do you entertain a feeling of endearment towards him. But once his words of praise have reached your ears, you rejoice in them and develop great love for the speaker. What is the reason for the hatred in the first example and for the love in the second one? It is only the contact between the senses and their objects.

Thus it becomes clear that the senses can enjoy peace, only when they do not come in contact with sense objects. In the alternative, one should be able to maintain a feeling of equanimity without giving way either to elation or agitation in spite of a contact between his senses and their objects and irrespective of whether the outcome of such a contact is pleasant or otherwise.

It should, however, be recognised that it is neither easy nor always possible to prevent the senses and their objects from coming into mutual contact. On the contrary, it is possible, with some effort, to develop an attitude of equipoise, notwithstanding such contacts which are more often unavoidable. To foster such an attitude, you should resort to the path of enquiry and thereby develop the firm conviction, "I am neither the body nor the sense organs. I am the ever-blissful Atma". Only when you are unshakeably established in this conviction, will the sense organs cease to trouble you. It is only through the pursuit of the path of enquiry accompanied by the constant contemplation on the idea that you are nothing other than the Atma that you can transcend the human limitations, and experience your Divine Self under all circumstances.

You may have heard about the great philosopher, Philip Sydney. As a boy, while he was staying away from his parents to attend his school in another town, his father wrote him a letter giving some words of advice as follows: "My dear son! Every day offer your heartfelt prayer to God. Always strive to turn your mind towards God. Conduct yourself with respect and humility towards your teachers and fellow students. Do not give room for anger, disappointment or discontentment. Don't get distressed when others criticise and abuse you or get elated when they praise you. Never criticise others". The father concluded his letter with the following important caution to his son,

"If ever you have to make a promise, make it only to God and to none else. Speech is God's gift. Hence you have no right to give a pledge to any one else. The plighted word should be offered only to God. If you follow this rule, you will grow in wisdom and your glory will shine. Always exercise control over your tongue and never allow it to run amuck. Thus you will stand forth as an ideal student in society". Philip Sydney scrupulously followed his father's advice and achieved great eminence as a philosopher.

Students should note that too much of talking is harmful to their mind. They should not concern themselves with any matters other than their studies. They must remember that they are seekers of knowledge and not seekers of extraneous things. Only after finishing your studies, can you engage yourselves in other activities. Even then you should be guided by the rule of moderation; never exceed the limits either in talking or in other matters relating to your daily life. The tongue is prone to four types of lapses: 1) Uttering lies, 2) Carrying tales against others, 3) Criticising or scandalising others, 4) Excessive talking. It is these four tendencies that deprive man of his peace of mind. One should speak the truth only. Of course, in some rare cases, it may be dangerous to speak the truth. Under such circumstances, you should be discreet enough to avoid speaking either truth or untruth. Only thus can you be a success in society.

The senses are extremely powerful. They are the root cause for all the joys and sorrows of mankind. You should, therefore, try to understand thoroughly the nature and role of the senses and harness them to your best advantage. An eminent poet sang thus about the havoc that the senses are capable of: "If the head harbours wicked thoughts, if the tongue indulges in calumny, if the eyes are keen to observe others' lapses, if the ears are alert to overhear others, if the mind and heart are bent upon deceiving others, - at the very sight of these monstrosities, justice and fair play will not survive at all".

Man's stronghold should be to adhere to the path of truth, rectitude and justice. But man's tragedy is that he becomes a helpless victim of his five senses which lead him astray and land him in endless problems. We have the classic examples of each kind of animal or insect being trapped and even losing its life on account of its weakness for one sense alone - the deer for the sense of sound, the elephant for the sense of touch, the moth for the sense of sight, the fish for the sense of taste, and the bee for the sense of smell. Hence, one can easily imagine the plight of man who is the unfortunate victim of all the five senses. In this context, the students should follow the shining example of the young devotee Prahlada. Despite all the tempting allurements designed by his father, despite all the ingeneous tutoring by his teachers at the instance of his father, and despite all the intimidations and tortures, as well as all the cruel attempts to kill him outright, Prahlada never succumbed to the sensual ways of worldly life, but struck tenanciously to the spiritual path only, with the Lord's name ever dancing on his tongue. He even used to lead his fellow-students also on the spiritual path, inspiring them with his melodious devotional songs and stories. Here is a sample of an interesting story which he had learnt from the Sage Narada and which he narrated to his young friends:

There was a king who had many wives. He had no peace of mind because of them. One day he wanted to find out whether there was any man in his entire kingdom who was free from worries due to a nagging wife. So after giving wide publicity, he arranged two big tents (pandals), the first one for those who were under their wives' control and the second one for those who had control over their wives. By the time of sunset, it was noticed that the first tent was filled to capacity, whereas there was not a single man in the second tent. At last one man came suddenly and sat in the second tent. The king felt happy that there was at least one man who had control over his wife. He met him inside the tent and asked him courteously to speak the truth as to whether he had control over his wife. The man replied that he would never speak a lie and that the truth was that he was squarely under his wife's control. The king then told him about the impropriety of his sitting in the wrong tent and ordered him to go and stand in the other tent. That hen-pecked husband replied in agony, "Your Majesty! I have strict orders from my wife to sit in this tent only at any cost. I dare not disobey her and go to the other tent, whatever punishment you may give me or even if you take my life". The lesson of this story is the mind which is supposed to be the husband of his wives, namely the senses, is in the pitiable plight of being a helpless slave to them. In fact, the order of control based on the increasing order of subtlety ought to be as follows: the body, the sense organs, the mind, the intellect and the Atma, each of them controlling the preceding one. This means that the Atma being the subtlest of all, should hold sway over the rest of them.

Since the sense organs are highly potent, the first and foremost task for man is to bring them under his control for leading an ideal life. Because young people today have lost control over their senses, all their actions and behaviour are devious. They do not know how to sit properly in the class-room, how to walk about, how to read, how to sleep and how to behave towards their parents,

61

teachers, elders and friends. They betray lack of concentration even while talking to somebody, by casting their looks hither and thither. They make unncessary gestures and odd movements of all their limbs as if they are dancing while engaged in conversation or speech making. While walking on the road, students should have their eyes on their feet so as to avoid distractions and prevent accidents. While sleeping they should stretch their body straight and not curl themselves like a coil of wire, which is bundled. By constant practice of the right way of doing things they will develop good habits and acquire mastery over all their senses.

Students should avoid unnecessary curiosity in respect of matters which do not directly concern them. If they indulge in excessive talk with all and sundry or if they go on interfering in others' affairs, they will make themselves unpopular and unwanted by others. Everybody will try to avoid such people and thus they will lose the respect of all. It is a very bad habit for students to be standing and talking in the bazaar. If at all talking is necessary, they should do it in their hostel rooms but never in the market place. The observance of discipline in all these matters is of paramount importance to the students.

To-day young people do not know how to sit properly while reading or writing etc. They sit with their backs bent and drooping like 80 year old people. This causes various ailments and leads to premature old age. While walking or sitting, you must be straight like a rod, keeping the spine erect. There is a physiological reason for this. A very important nerve called the Sushumna Naadi, runs through the spinal column, from its base in the Mooladhara to the Sahasraara at top of the head. If this gets bent, serious results will follow. The importance of the Sushumna Naadi is known only to those engaged in the practice of Kundalini Yoga.

When the situation requires, we should not hesitate to carry our footwear. For instance, when we have to cross a rivulet on foot, or if it rains heavily when we are walking, it is convenient to carry our shoes. Although the worth of the footwear is very little, we should give due respect to it, because it protects our feet when required. Here is a story about how and why Sri Krishna carried the shoes of a woman. On the ninth day of the Kurukshetra war, Bhishma, the Commander of the Kaurava Army took a serious vow that he would kill all the Pandava brothers in the next day's battle. Draupadi, the wife of the Pandavas, came to know about this. In her great anxiety and worry, she ran to Sri Krishna, fell at His feet and prayed to Him to save the lives of her five husbands. It was 10 p.m. then. Sri Krishna hit upon a strategy. He asked Draupadi to hasten to the tent of Bhishma and prostrate before him making sure that there is jingling of her bangles in the process of prostration. Further he asked her to leave her footwear with him and go to Bhishma with bare feet, because if she went with her footwear, Bhishma would be alerted by the sound of her footwear and might recognise her, in which case, His strategy of getting her blessed by Bhishma would not succeed.

According to Krishna's advice, Draupadi with her head-veil went softly barefooted to Bhishma's tent. At that time Bhishma was restlessly walking to and fro in his tent. He was upset by a strong feeling of remorse about the vow he had taken on the battlefield that day to kill all the Pandavas in the next day's battle. He could not eat or sleep that night because his conscience told him that the

63

Pandavas were the very embodiment of Sathya and Dharma - Truth and Righteousness - and that it was therefore, a great sin on his part to kill them mercilessly without any justification. Engrossed in these thoughts he was pacing up and down when Draupadi entered the tent and swiftly prostrated before him, making a jingling sound with her bangles, as suggested by Krishna. Since the sound of bangles indicated that the woman was a "Sumangali" i.e., a woman whose husband was alive, Bhishma in accordance with the Hindu tradition and custom blessed her, saying, "Deergha Sumangali Bhava", which means "May you live long together with your husband(s)", not knowing the identity of the woman who was prostrating before him. Now Draupadi knew for certain that Bhishma's blessing would never go in vain. So, no sooner did she hear Bhishma's blessings than she joyously sprang to her feet and removing her head-veil thanked Bhishma profusely and told him that it was for the sake of this very blessing that she came to his tent at that odd hour. Bhishma was highly surprised when he discovered that it was Draupadi whom he had blessed in a manner which ran counter to the vow he had taken. Then he began questioning her, "Who has designed this strategy for you? Who has shown you the way to my tent? Has anybody accompanied you?"

As he was questioning her thus, Krishna made His dramatic apperance before Bhishma and Draupadi. It did not take Bhishma long to guess that Sri Krishna, the Master Strategist of the whole universe, was behind the entire plot and the scene being enacted in his tent. Beside himself with joyous excitement, Bhishma exclaimed, "O Lord Krishna! It is quite evident now that this is all your divine plan and your impeccably perfect game!" Bhishma now felt relieved of his sense of remorse and infact, he even felt glad about the whole affair, because it served the dual purpose of saving the lives of Pandavas on the one hand and saving himself on the other hand from the ignominy and sin of slaying the virtuous Pandavas.

Now that Bhishma was relieved of his tension and anxiety and became his normal self, he felt the pangs of hunger; because due to the worried state of his mind till a little while ago, he did not feel hungry and hence he had not eaten anything that night after that day's fierce fighting in the battlefield. He then noticed some packet which Krishna was carrying in his arm-pit. Thinking that it might be a packet of some eatables which could relieve his hunger, he eargerly enquired Krishna about the contents of the packet. The playful Krishna suddenly let go the packet from his arm-pit and when it got ripped while falling on the ground, what did Bhishma as well as Draupadi see to their utter amazement? Lo and behold, a pair of shoes! With a mischievous smile Krishna pointed His finger toward them saying, "They are Draupadi's slippers". Both Bhishma and Draupadi could not contain themselves, because, leave alone Bhishma, even Draupadi never expected or suspected that Krishna would carry her slippers. Both of them began shedding profuse tears of ecstasy at what the Lord did. Choked with emotion Bhishma exclaimed, "O Lord Krishna! Who can understand Your Divine Leelas? There is no limit to the troubles You undergo in order to protect Your devotees who have surrendered themselves at Your Lotus Feet. In order to save Your devotees, You never hesitate to do even such things which others would consider as demeaning, degrading or debasing. What a Merciful Lord You are!"

The lesson which the students should learn from this story is that they should not consider anything as mean and beneath their dignity, as long as it serves the purpose of helping the needy, without deviating however from the path of rectitude. Our ancient scriptures like the Vedas, Sastras, Puranas, - Mythological books - and Ithihasas - Epics - provide plenty of shining examples of people who led such noble and ideal lives. But the students of today are so ignorant about our scriptures that they do not know what is meant by Sastras, or Ramayana or Parayana - Recital of scriptures. Thus they are forfeiting the rich heritage of their glorious culture and tradition. Students of the Sai Educational system should, therefore, become pioneers in imbibing a judicious and harmonious combination of both secular and sacred learning i.e., acquiring both scientific and spiritual knowledge.

You hear people talking about "Culture" and "Spirituality" as if they are two different things. In My view, Culture is only the essence derived from Spirituality. Just as sugar is common to all the varieties of sweets which are seemingly different from one another, spirituality is common to the seemingly different cultures of all lands and nations. In short, you should recognise that culture is a part of the all-inclusive spirituality. you must cultivate and develop this all-inclusive unitary vision. The various organs and limbs of the body are not different from the body. Viswam-the universe - is not separate from Vishnu -God. Likewise, you have to recognise that what you call 'secular' and 'sacred' or 'worldly' and 'spiritual', are not two discrete and unrelated things, but only two facets of one indivisible Reality or Truth. This fact can be easily grasped by you, if you consider the example of a bean seed which consists of two cotyledons covered by a common seed-coat. When the bean seed is sown in the field, and when it germinates, you can see the sapling consisting of the two thick cotyledons with the plumule in between them. The seedling grows, deriving its nourishment from both the cotyledons. So also, the seedling called human being requires for his growth and full development both the secular and sacred aspects of life. These two aspects of life neither exist nor can they thrive independently in isolation from each other. They are both intimately and inextricably related. The sum-total of these two aspects is what you call "Culture". People lacking in such broad-minded unitary vision see the apparent and even imaginary differences between the culture of one nation and another. True wisdom lies in discerning and discovering the fundamental unity behind the superficial differences in the world culture. The same thing applies to the concept of religions too. To say that Hinduism, Budhism, Christianity, Islam etc. are different religions, betrays not only narrow-mindedness but also the lack of understanding about the meaning of "religion". "Religion" means "Realisation". Since realisation is one and the same, irrespective of whatever religion is professed by different men, it logically follows that basically all religions are one; or to be more accurate, there is only one religion.

In this connection, there is a small story. When Krishna went to Dhritarashtra as an ambassador on behalf of the Pandavas, Dhritarashtra asked Him, " O Krishna! Pandavas and Kauravas are the sons of two brothers. Being Divine, why are you partial to the Pandavas? Why don't you love the Kauravas, too? Krishna replied, "O King, I am sorry to say that you are blind not only physically but also spiritually. You should understand that I cannot but support and help those who take refuge in Me and who surrender to Me without any reservation. The celestial Sage, Narada once asked Narayana about His correct address, as He had many "branch Offices". Narayana answered Narada saying that His "Head Office" or permanent address where He stayed always was the heart of the devotee who constantly remembered Him with supreme love and devotion. Apart form this, let me tell you the nature of relationship between the Pandavas and Myself. Dharmaja is My head, Arjuna My shoulder, Bhima My stomach, Nakula and Sahadeva My legs. I am the heart. hence we are all inseparable parts of one and the same body."

The implication of the above reply of Krishna, in answer to Dhritarashtra, is that the body, the senses, the mind, the intellect and the Atma together constitute the integral human personality, illustrating the truth of the Vedic declaration "Ekam Sath", i.e. "Existence is One". Just as the body has several parts, the one Lord has also several names.

Students! Till now, in this Summer Course, you have been told about the body and the senses and their relationship. From tomorrow, we shall consider the inter-relationship between the mind and the senses, between the intellect and the senses, as well as the Atmic Principle that runs as the common under-current which integrates and animates the entire human system.

Hold the Reins

Mind alone is the cause
For man's rise and fall in life;
Mind alone is responsible
For man's bondage or liberation;
This mind alone makes man forget
his reality and land himself in hell!

Dear Students!

Man is a combination of body, mind and Atma. These three together constitute the steps for man's ascent to the highest stage.The body is the instrument for actions. The Mind is concerned with cognition. The changeless and permanent Reality is the Atma, which is the divine aspect of man. Thus, doing, knowing and being are the triune manifestations of the human personality. Although the body, mind and Atma have different names and characteristics, their harmonization and unification help man to raise himself from the human to the divine level. On the contrary, their alienation from one another degrades him to the animal level.

The word "Antahkarana" - inner instrument is used in every-day worldly context as well as in the spiritual parlance. What is its form, its nature, its role, its importance and its destination? When we enquire along these lines, it will be found that mind itself assumes the subtle form of Antahkarana, consisting of four aspects,namely, Manas - mind, Buddhi - intellect, Chitta - memory, and Ahamkara - ego, the last three being the subtle aspects of the mind. The particular name is given, based on the functions performed, just as one and the same brahmin is called a priest - Pujari when he performs worship in a temple, a cook when he works in the kitchen, a teacher when he teaches students, and a "Panchaanga Brahmin" when he interprets the almanc - panchaanga.

In the same manner when the mind is engaged in wavering thought processes, it is called Manas. When is it busy in the process of enquiry and discrimination between right and wrong, it is named as Buddhi - intellect. When it functions as a repository of memories, it is known as Chitta. When it identifies itself with the physical body, assuming the doership for various activities, it goes by the name of Ahamkara - ego. Thus, it may be seen that the mind, although basically one, displays these varied forms on account of the different roles assumed by it. In fact, the mind alone is the cause of all things. "Manomoolam idam Jagat" say the Scriptures. It means the whole cosmos is nothing but a projection of the mind.

Man derives his name from the possession of the mind. As a man thinks, so he becomes. Man means mind, and mind means man. Mind is only a bundle of thoughts. Thoughts give rise to actions, and what we enjoy or suffer in this world are the consequences of these actions.It follows, therefore, that only when man's thoughts are good, his life will be good. Thoughts are highly potent. They survive the death of man. Hence it is essential to keep out bad thoughts from our minds. It is bad thoughts which separate man from man and make them forget their common divinity. When men realise that the Atma in every body is one and the same, there will be no room for differences. Man should try to expand his relationship gradually from the individual level to the level of the family, the community, the nation and finally the whole world. The peace of the individual as well as of the world depends on the mind. hence the need for proper disciplining of the mind. Like a fish swimming against the current to save itself from dangers, man should combat the evil thoughts within and protect himself from dangers.

Man to-day is creating all sorts of trouble for himself, because of his wrong thoughts. None else should be blamed for his pleasures or pains, gains or losses. Mind is the root of the tree of Samsara - cycle of births and deaths, and the manifested universe in general. To destroy this tree, the axe should be laid at the root itself. In other words, the mind should be destroyed by diverting the thoughts to the enquiry about the Atma - the real Self or the real 'I'.

Based on the differences in the nature of the mind, different colours are attributed to it. For instance, the mind filled with anger is red in colour. A selfish mind is wheat-brown. An egotistic mind is of the orange hue, while the mind dedicated to god is pure white.

To-day the world is riddled with fear. Whether at home, or out in the street, or while travelling in a train, bus or plane, people are haunted by fear. The root cause for this ubiquitous fear is the absence of pure and sacred thoughts in the minds of men. The whole world appears like a maze filled with fear at every turn. The tragedy of Abhimanyu - son of Arjuna and a hero of Kurukshetra war was that he knew how to enter the maze called Padmavyuha but he knew not how to get out of it. Likewise, you know how to enter the maze of worldly pleasures, but do not know how to get out of it. You will know the way out only when you submit your thoughts to the scrutiny of the Buddhi - intellect.

In the Kathopanishad, the body is compared to a chariot, the senses to horses, the mind to the reins, and the intellect

71

to the charioteer. This means that the mind is in between the senses and the intellect. If the mind follows the dictates of the intellect, it will be safe. If, on the contrary, it follows the whims and fancies of the senses, it will become a bondslave of the senses and a victim of endless sorrow and suffering. Allowing free rein to the senses is the Pravritthi Marga - the external path, while controlling the senses is the Nivritthi Marga - the internal path. Most people are content to pursue the external. Few are concerned to explore the internal. Many people to-day employ their thoughts and efforts in harming others. They do not realise the fact that the harm they do to others will recoil on themselves many fold. An outstanding example of this is the vicious Kauravas led by Duryodhana and Dussasana subjecting the virtuous Pandavas to innumerable hardships. What was the ultimate result of this? Although the Pandavas suffered temporarily, in the final reckoning the Kauravas were utterly destroyed for ever. Students! Always remember this and never think of hurting others. Don't criticise or condemn others. If you deceive your friends, they in turn will cheat you. If you disobey your parents, your children will pay you back in the same coin. If your hurt others, they will hurt you in retaliation. This kind of reaction, resound and reflection are inherent in man's mind. Hence you should scrupulously follow the maxim : "Hurt never; help ever". There are some sinful persons who cavil not only at other men, but even against God. This seems to be their very nature, although God never harms any one at any time.

In this context, the lowest category of people are those who take sadistic pleasure in hurting other people without any provocation whatsoever. They may be compared to the moths whose nature is to damage all clothes indiscriminately - whether it is a valuable saree costing one thousand rupees, or whether it is a worthless soiled rag in the kitchen. This highly despicable tendency on the part of some persons to harm others, is traceable to their bad thoughts. We try to dispel foul odours from our living rooms and toilets by using substances like air-fresheners, incense sticks, and other deodorants. Similarly we should try to counteract our bad thoughts with good ones. Good thoughts will eventually lead us to the fulfilment of our lifes, while bad thoughts will degrade us to the level of beasts. No doubt, the replacement of bad thoughts by good ones, calls for sincere and determined effort, because as Arjuna complained to Krishna the mind is fickle - Chanchalam, turbulent - Pramathi, strong - Balavath and stubborn - Dridham.

Everyone clamours for peace. But peace is not anywhere outside; it is right there within us only. However, if you want to enjoy that peace, you have to resort to practice - Abhyasa; what type of practice? First of all give up selfish thoughts. Then persistently engage yourself in the constant enquiry of what your really are. If you merely repeat thrice, saying " I am a man. I am a man. I am a man", you will be half-a-man only. To realise your manhood in full, you should also repeat, " I am not an animal, I am not an animal, I am not an animal". For, people now-a-days call themselves men, but behave as animals. In the light of this fact, the animal is better than the man, because the animal thinks of itself as an animal and behaves accordingly, whereas man claims himself to be a man but behaves like an animal! You got the name "Man" because you are endowed with Manas-mind. However to deserve that name, you should mould your mind in the proper manner which befits a man but not a beast.

Mind is a priceless possession. it is God's greatest gift to man. The Scriptures have declared that the mind alone is responsible either for man's bondage or for his liberation. So, how can you condemn the mind as bad, when it is capable of leading you to the supreme goal of liberation? A knife can be used to cut fruits and vegetables. But in a fit of anger and frustration, if you make use of it for cutting your own throat or others' throats, is it the fault of the knife? Likewise, you cannot blame the mind, if you misuse it. Whether the mind contributes to your upliftment or downfall depends on how you use. it.

The mind is often compared to a cat. A cat gently catches hold of its young kitten with its mouth and carries them from place to place to ensure their safety and nourishment. In utter contrast, the cat uses the same mouth for fiercely pouncing upon rats and tearing them to pieces. Similar is the case with the mind. It serves as the supreme benefactor of those, who engage themselves in the contemplation of God, in good thoughts, good words and good actions. On the other hand, the same mind brings disaster to those who take to the wrong path of unrigtheousness or outright wickedness.

The way in which the mind functions may also be likened to mono-acting. Because, one and the same mind assumes different forms and plays different roles, depending on the needs of varying situations.

In the beginningless beginning God was one. The thought arose in Him " I am one; let Me become many", and thus the One became the many. However, despite the many, the unity still persists unaffected by the diversity. Thus, whether for the unity in diversity, or for the diversity in unity, only thoughts -Samkalpas are responsible. What is needed is to regulate our thoughts in the right manner. As soon as a thought arises, we should not rush into action, but should subject the thought to the scrutiny of the intellect for a correct decision before implementing the thought. But now-a-days most people have the tendency to be in a hurry to put their thoughts into action without any such deliberation. That is the reason for the statement, "Haste makes waste, waste makes worry, so do not be in hurry". Therefore, action undertaken after deliberation alone results in peace.

People talk of world peace. But how can you ensure peace in the world? Here is the formula for it. "If there is righteousness in the heart, there will be beauty in the character. If there is beauty in the character, there will be harmony in the home. If there is harmony in the home, there will be order in the nation. If there is order in the nation, there will be peace in the world". It may thus be seen that the first link in the chain leading to world peace is righteousness or Dharma. Dharma is only another name for right action. But the pre-requisite for right action is right thought. In other words, peace should start with the individual and gradually spread wider and wider right along the line - from the home or family to the village to the nation, etc., till finally, it encompasses the entire world.

You chant, "Peace, Peace, Peace" - i. e., three times after meditation, Bhajan etc. By merely uttering thrice with your tongue, you cannot obtain or ensure peace. The significance of the three chants is that man is in need or three kinds of peace : (i) Adhibhoutik - peace unhampered by other beings, (ii) Adhyatmik - peace undisturbed by ones' own body and mind, (iii) Adhidaivik - peace undisturbed by forces beyond human control. Of these three, "Adhi-daivi" signifies the need for Divine Grace which can be earned only by absolute surrender to God. This concept of "surrender to God" is often misunderstood. Surrender does not mean the abandonment of all activities, foolishly thinking that "God will do whatever is necessary for me, because I have

75

surrendered everything to Him'. That would be sheer laziness. It is like sitting before a plate of chapatis with potato curry, and idly expecting your hunger to be satisfied without eating the stuff. On the other hand, the correct meaning of surrender is to make use of your God-given faculties and energy to perform your legitimate work, dedicating all your activities to the Lord, without the false sense of doership and without undue concern for the results of your actions.

Students! If your want to have good thoughts, you must resort to the spiritual path. The starting point for spiritual path is Satsang - holy company.

Thoughts are contagious. Hence the adage, "Tell me your company, and I will tell you what you are". You should therefore, scrupulously eschew bad company. Shri Shankara has eulogized the vlaue of holy company in glowing terms as follows : "The company of the wise begets detachment, detachment leads to the destruction of delusion, followed by the acquisition of steady wisdom, and culminating finally in Jivanmukti- liberation, while alive". Therefore, the essential point you should remember is that only good company will engender good thoughts in you.

Students! Cultivate and develop only sacred thoughts and thus sanctify your lives. Become ideal men, so that others may also derive the benefit by following your example. Bad company, bad thoughts and sensuous ways of living may give you momentary pleasure but will eventually drown you in untold misery and utter ruin. Remember that you cannot but reap what you sow. When you are born from your mother's womb, your neck is not bedecked with flower garlands or with necklaces of gold, pearls or diamonds; but be rest assured that your neck does carry on it an unseen heavy garland given by Brahma -, the

76

Creator - the garland of the fruits of good and bad actions done by you in previous lives.

Let me conclude with a word about gratitude. For want of gratitude, man is degrading himself to a lower level than even the animals. You say "thanks" to some body who picks up and gives to you your own hand-kerchief which you happened to drop on the ground. But how very strange and surprising that you never think of thanking God for all the precious things He has so graciously bestowed on you! He has placed you in this vast and wonderful universe, providing for you pure air to breathe, clean water to drink, mother earth to live on, etc. In short, but for the five great elements created by Him, you cannot live even for a moment. Therefore, is there a greater sin than forgetting to offer your thanks to such an all-merciful God?

You buy a plot of land with your own money and construct a house thereon with your own money. But the Corporation wants you to pay the house-tax, just for providing electricity and water, of course levying separate additional taxes for these amenities. But tell me, what tax are you paying to God for providing you with facilities like the sun who illumines the whole world, the wind which refreshes all living beings with cool breeze, the torrential rain that not only cools the earth but also sustains life, and so on and so forth? Not to give any thought to such things, indicates not only ingratitude on the part of man but also the Tamoguna -inertia that is polluting his mind.

Vagaries of the Mind

It is the mind that matters, wherever one may be,
Neither home nor forest can give you liberation;
It makes no difference - whether you are in the
temple or forest,
As long as the mind is not up to the mark.

Dear students!

"The universe is like the reflection of a city in a mirror", declared Dakshinamurthy. What man has to achieve primarily is the purification and final annihilation of the Antahkarana - inner instrument - not so much the Purusharthas, viz., Dharma - Righteousness, Artha - Wealth, Kama -Fulfilment of desires and Moksha - Liberation. The whole world along with its joys and sorrows, vices and virtues, truth and untruth, justice and injustice etc is in the mind only.

The mind is like a clean mirror. It has no intrinsic power of its own to directly experience the sense objects except through the concerned sense organs. For instance, it can see only through the eyes and hear only through the ears but can neither see nor hear by itself independently. Consequently, the offences committed by the the senses are reflected in the mirror of mind. No blame attaches to the mind *per se*. It is the association with the wayward senses that pollutes the mind. According to the Scriptures, the mind is subject to three kinds of pollution : Mala, Vikshepa and Avarana.

What is Mala? Man commits many offences, knowingly or unknowinlgy, not only in this life but also in previous lives. The imprint of these actions is carried by the Chitta - memory life after life, like the dust accumulating on the surface of a mirror day after day. Thus the mirror of man's mind gets covered up by such dirt, which is technically named as "Mala". On account of this Mala, man is unable to see clearly the reflection of his real identity in the mirror of his mind. Hence, it is necessary to cleanse the mirror of the impurities covering it. This cleansing is done by regulating one's food and other living habits including recreation. Young students particularly should strictly avoid eating impure food. Purity should be ensured with regard to the vessels used for cooking - patra suddhi, the food materials used for cooking - padaartha suddhi, and thirdly, the process of cooking -paaka suddhi. In this connection, an important point which is generally overlooked is the fact that many of the ills from which people suffer to-day are due to consuming things obtained through unfair means as well as polluted by the bad vibrations from cooks of questionalbe character. It is extremely difficult, if not altogether impossible especially in the present-day context, to ensure such purity in all these respects and at all times. To get over these practical difficulties, the way-out suggested by the Scriptures is to offer the food to God before eating it, duly regarding it as God's gift. To the question "Where is God"?, the answer is given in verse 14 of Chapter 15 of the Gita - "Aham Vaiswanaro bhutva" etc - which declares that the Lord dwells in every one as Vaiswanara - the digestive fire and digests the different kinds of food that is consumed. If you eat food without first offering it to God, you will be affected by all the impurities and defects present in it. On the contrary, if you offer the food to the Lord before eating, as suggested in verse 24 of Chapter 4 of the Gita "Brahmaarpanam"etc it becomes Prasada - Gift from God, and consequently all the impurities in the food are thereby eliminated. This helps the process of gradually cleansing the mind of its impurity or dirt called Mala. It should, however, be borne in mind that the complete removal of Mala cannot be done in a day or a month. This requires persistent and prolonged practice. If raw gold or ore is to be converted into pure gold, it has to be melted on fire repeatedly to remove the impurities. So also the impurity of man's mind, called "Mala" can be eleminated only by constant practice over a period of time.

The second distortion of the mind called Vikshepa is due the constant wavering of the mind, like the movements of the reflected image in a mirror that is kept moving or shaking frequently. To control this waywardness of the mind, one should undertake various spiritual practices like meditation, prayer and the nine modes of devotion mentioned in the Scriptures, viz., 1. Sravanam - listening to the Lord's stories, Leelas and Mahima, 2. Kirtanam - singing His glories, 3. Smaranam - remembrance. 4. Pada Sevanam - service to the Lotus Feet, 5. Archanam - worship, 6. Vandanam - salutation, 7. Daasyam - master - servant relationship. 8. Sakhyam - companionship. 9. AtmaNivedanam - offering oneself to the Lord i.e, Self -surrender.

If the young students of to-day who will be the leaders of Bharat tomorrow, cannot control the fickleness of their minds, and cleanse the impurities thereof, the future administration and politics of the country cannot but be deplorably impure and corrupt. Students should realise that education is for life but not for making out a livelihood. They should strain their every nerve to acquire steadiness of mind, which is a prerequisite for concentration. For this, you should bend the body, mend the senses, and end the mind and this is the process of attaining immortality. If you want to be masters and not slaves, you should keep your body, senses and mind under your control.

Why is the country to-day torn by srife, indiscipline, violence and chaos? Because people, both young and old, are pre-occupied with external material things, totally ignoring the spirit within. The entire educational system is riddled with selfishness. Educated persons want to amass wealth quickly by any means, fair or foul, hook or crook. It is the same motive that is impelling many students to go abroad and acquire money for selfish ends, without any regard for their parents or their mother-land. Such self -centred intellectuals who suffer from the craze to go abroad should remember the declaration of the Scriptures that "one's mother and motherland are much superior even to heaven". They should give up their obsession for acquiring wealth and realise that real wealth consists in leading virtuous lives coupled with love and service to the land of their birth. Your foremost duty is to show gratitude to your parents to whom you owe everything including your food, blood and head. You have to take care of them, especially in their old age. If you discharge your duties properly and lead your lives on these lines which broaden and purify your minds and hearts, your mind will automatically become free from the distortion of Vikshepa and you will acquire steadiness and concentration of mind without the need for any other spiritual disciplines.

Now, we come to the third distortion of the mind: Avarana. This may be likened to a thick cloth covering the mirror of man's mind, which does not at all permit of any reflection whatsoever of the image of the Self. Thus, while Mala does not enable us to have a clear and correct image of the Self, and while Vikshepa results in seeing the Self as wavering, Avarana altogether hides the Reality - Self-and makes one identify himself wrongly with his body.

Students! Recognise that what you are experiencing as the real world is only the "Reaction", "Resound" and "Reflection" of your "Real Self". Now, the question arises,

81

"What exactly is the thick cloth that covers the mirror of one's mind"? This cloth is made up of the Arishadvarga - the gang of six internal enemies of man - viz. Kama - Desire, Krodha -Anger, Lobha -Greed, Moha - attachemnt, Mada - Pride, Maatsarya - Jealousy, Envy. Out of the six, Pride may be considered as the worst enemy. Pride is of eight kinds - pride of money, learning, caste, affluence, beauty, youth, position or authority and Tapas - Spiritual pride. If you ponder over two facts you can overcome this enemy namely pride.

Firstly, if you look around instead of being like a frog in the well, you will find that in respect of each of these eight items which cause pride in you, there are many other people who are superior to you. Secondly, all these items - money, authority, youth etc. - are highly transient. Therefore, get rid of pride as well as the other five enemies included in the Arishadvarga, if you want to remove the Avarana covering your mind's mirror. The best means to remove this thick cloth of Avarana is to develop love for all. Love is God. Live in Love.

Love is the only bond that can unite all and make us realise the one Reality behind all the seeming diversity. A simple illustration will make this point clear. You have a candle light. You cover it with a vessel having several holes in it. Although there is one light, you see light through each and every hole, giving the impression of there being several lights. Now, you cover the vessel with a thick cloth. You see no light at all. Next you remove the thick cloth. You see many lights again. Now break or remove the pot. You see the one and only real candle light.

Similarly, the Atma inside you is covered by the body having nine holes thorough which you see the multiplicity and diversity in the world. You have covered this nine-holed body of yours with a thick cloth which is woven with the warp and woof of 'I' or Ahamkara and "Mine-Mamakara", when you remove the cloth made up of 'I' and 'Mine', and when you get rid of the wrong identification with the body, the Avarana of the mind disappears, and you see the light of your Real Self - the Atma Jyoti, the only Light-Eka Jyothi, dispelling the darkness of the illusory multiplicity.

The mind, the intellect, the memory and ego which together constitute the Antahkarana - the inner instrument - are formless but the external instruments, the sense organs, which are the media through which the Antahkarana perceives the phenomenal world, have forms. The Antahkarana is subject to four kinds of defects, viz., Bhranthi - Delusion, Pramadam - Hazard or Danger, Kar-anaapaatavam - weakness of the instruements, and Vipralipsa - Jealousy. These four defects result in the mal-function-ing of the Antahkarana.

Bhranthi refers to the deluded state of mind in which a person mistakes, for instance, a rope for a snake and *vice versa*. In other words, he regards the unreal as real, and the real as unreal; the temporary as permanent and the permanent as temporary.

Such delusions invariably lead to accidents or dangerous situations - "Pramaadam". If you hold a snake thinking it is a rope, you are certainly in for trouble. Man to-day regards the body as real, not knowing that it is as unreal as a water bubble, which is sure to burst at any time, at any place.

Students! You must carefully note one point. If it is the sense organs that enable a man to see, hear, talk and so on, how is it that even when all the organs are there intact in a dead person, he is unable to see, hear, talk etc? It is because the power that aminates the organs is not there. The body may be compared to a torch light. The eyes are like the bulbs. The intellect is the switch. If with all these, you dont' get light, what could be the reason? Obviously there are no battery cells inside. The blood cells in our body are like those battery cells. They carry the Divine energy in them. The blood cells may be there, but if the divine power has left them, they can no longer make the senses function. So it is clear that in the presence of the divine power the body can do many wonders; in its absence, the body becomes not only inert, but also decomposed and rotten.

Once a Vedantin came to Me and asked, "Swami! Sankaracharya has said that Brahman alone is real and the world is illusory. But we are directly perceiving the world as substantial and deriving so many experiences from it. How can we deny its existence?" I told him, ?My dear one! Leave to the world itself the question of its reality or unreality. First of all, find out whether you are real or unreal". Like that Vedantin, the students of today also want to learn about everything else but not about their own reality. You seem to be more concerned with the "news" outside than the "nuisance" inside you. First get rid of this nuisance of your ignorance; realise your true nature. reform yourself first, before thinking of reforming others. Otherwise, your Bhrama - delusion will land you in Pramaadam - danger.

The third defect of the mind, Karana apaatavam means weakness or debility of the instruments. This weakness affects both the inner instrument - Antahkarana and the external instruments - the sense organs. Here is a small story to illustrate the weakness of Antahkarana. There was a rich farmer in a village. He was the undisputed leader of the village. There was another middle-class farmer in the same village. One day the cattle belonging to both these farmers were grazing together. Unexpectedly there started a fierce fighting between the two bullocks, one belonging to the rich farmer, and the other to the middle-class farmer. During the fight, the rich man's bullock died due to the injury to some vital and vulnerable part of its body. Now, the middle -class farmer who was there at that time became deeply worried. He ran to the village to inform the rich farmer about the fatal accident to the latter's bullock. But due to the highly nervous and confused state of his mind, he was tremebling with fear and he told the rich farmer that the latter's bullock had killed the bullock of the former; i. e. the opposite of what actually happened. The rich farmer very calmly received the news. He consoled the small farmer, saying that, when human being endowed with intelligence are killing each other, there is no wonder if the rich farmer's bullock has killed the small farmer's bullock, because after all the animals are devoid of any intelligence; in the meanwhile, the small farmer realised his mistake in giving a wrong report and told the rich man, "Respected Sir, I have unwittingly committed a blunder by giving a wrong version of the accident. I am very sorry to tell you that it is my bullock that has killed your bullock. On hearing this, the rich man was beside himself with anger. He rebuked and abused the small farmer in very strong terms and demanded from him a penalty of five hundered rupees. This story betrays the "Karana-apaatavam", in respect of the rich man's Antahkarana which obviously was weak because of its inconsistent behaviour based on the feeling of "I" and "Mine" as opposed to the "other" man.

Now, let us consider some examples of "Karana-apaatvam" relating to the external instruments the sense organs.When a person is suffering from malarial fever, even Laddu -delicious sweet - will taste bitter. This is due to the diseased condition of the tongue but not due to any defect in Laddu. Similarly, a jaundiced eye will see everything as yellow, irrespective of whether the actual colour is white, red or black etc. It must, however, be noted that the ailments of the external instruments have an adverse effect on the internal instruments, because of their relatedness. Anyway, the net effect of Karana apaatavam as a whole, is to undermine Maanavatwa - human nature.

The fourth deficiency of the Antahkarana is "Vipralipsa" which means jealousy or envy. It is one of the worst qualities of man. He cannot endure or tolerate the prosperity or happiness of others. There is no cure for this disease. Feel happy when others are happy. Do not give room for envy. Develop fraternal feelings towards your fellow students. Rejoice in their curricular and extra-curricular achievements, without any feeling of envy. The reason for envy is selfishness, which is rampant now-a-days both among the students and non-students. For instance, ablebodied students rush in and occupy the front seats in buses, even pushing aside the old people, women and children who are standing in a long queue. Why don't you give preference to such people? Even if you don't get a seat in the bus, you can afford to walk a mile or two, thereby deriving the double benefit of saving the bus fare and giving much needed exercise to your body.

Students! All that you have to do to achieve purity in thought, word and deed is to follow these five injuctions

> *Think no evil; think what is good.*
> *See no evil; see what is good.*
> *Hear no evil; hear what is good*
> *Talk no evil; talk what is good*
> *Do no evil; do what is good.*

When you adhere to these five injunctions as the very breath of your life, you will be able to overcome all the four defects of the Antahkarana and achieve purity of mind and the other three components of the Antahkarana, and thereby experience ineffable bliss.

Students! You are aware that water is stored in tanks during the rainy season, and its used later on during summer to irrigate the agricultural lands. Similarly, from this moment you should cultivate control of the body, the senses and the Antahkarna, because now you have the vigour and vitality of youth. Acquire God's Grace in abundance now, when the time is opprotune. It will stand you in good stead in your future which will then be bright, secure and prosperous. Also remember that God will never forget His devotees. It is the devotees who forget God. God never forsakes His devotees; only the devotees forsake God.

Students! The body, the mind and the senses are like water taps, while the intellect is like the water tank. As is the water in the tank, so is the water in the taps. So, in the days ahead, we shall be discussing about this important faculty of Buddhi-intellect.

Buddhi the Charioteer

Purity of mind is the pathway to progress,
Purity of mind means mighty power;
A pure mind is like a precious pearl in the sea;
Never forget these words of wisdom.

See no evil, speak no evil;
Hear no evil - anytime, anywehre, in the world;
Remember always the picture of the three monkeys;
What I say is truth, indeed!

You have been told previously that, according to the Upanishads, the human body is a chariot, the sense organs being the horses, with the mind as the reins. However beautiful the chariot may be, however dependable the horses, however firm and secure the reins, all of these are of no use, if there is no charioteer. So also, however efficient the body, the senses and the mind may be, they serve no purpose in the absence of the choriteer, namely, Buddhi-intellect. In life's journey, the intellect is of supreme importance. It is called Nischayatmika Buddhi, which means, that the Buddhi has the decision making capacity. In daily life, many difficulties, problems and disturbances arise from time to time. For overcoming all these obstacles, Buddhi is our manistay. Without the intervention of the Buddhi, none of our problems can be solved. "Samsayaatma vinasyathi", says the Gita, which means that a man filled with doubts will perish. Because the Buddhi destroys doubts, the Gita affirms, "Buddhi grahayam athindriyam" - Buddhi can grasp that which is beyond the grasp of the sense organs.

The Bhagavad Gita has laid down two banks to channalise its message. In the absence of these banks, the river of life will be subject to many problems, difficulties and hazards. The two banks are symbolised by two Mantras.

One is "Sraddhavaan labhathe Jnanam - the man of faith acquires supreme wisdom. The other is: Samsayaatma vinasyathi - the one filled with doubts will perish. When the river of life flows in between these two banks of Mantras, it will be blessed with peace and happiness and ultimately reach the sea of Divine Grace which is its goal.

"Antarvaani" - inner voice is another name for the Buddhi. Man is guided by this inner voice in the conduct of his life. Whenever problems arise, he awaits the directives of the inner voice. If satisfactory answers are not forthcoming from his inner voice, man will have no satisfaction in life. In other words, his satisfaction with the external world is a function of his satisfaction with his inner world represented by the inner voice. Sometimes you hear people saying , "My conscience is not satisfied; or my conscience does not approve of this". Here conscience referes to the inner voice. So when you are exhorted to "Follow the Master", the Master stands for your conscience. Only when you follow the dictates of your conscience can you reach the right destination.

The name Vijnana is also sometimes attributed to the Buddhi. But it is not correct, because Vijnana means the so-called scientific or mundane knowledge which helps man to discover facts relating to the objective or phenomenal world, whereas Buddhi is concerned with the subtle realm of the inner world. Hence the role of the Buddhi should be correctly understood.

Off and on, the Buddhi tends to be covered by Ahamkara - the ego sense. In this context, one should remember that the senses are subtler than the body, the mind is even more subtle than the senses, and the Buddhi far more subtle than the mind. The Atma, of course, is subtlest of all. In the light of this fact, when we say that Ahamkaara is able

89

to envelope the Buddhi, it means that Ahamkara is subtler than the Buddhi. Thus, Ahamkara, being extremely subtle, is all-pervasive. and permeates all our actions. This is why man is unable to transcend Ahamkara and experience the Atma - the Self.

Once a king summoned an assembly of great scholars to his court. He posed the following question before them: " You are all distinguished scholars who have mastered the scriptures. Can you tell me how many among you are capable of attaining liberation?" Despite all their academic learning, none of the Pundits had the courage to stand up and give an affirmative answer. The whole assembly was stunned into silence. At that stage, an ordinary man from among the public got up and said boldly: (In Telugu), Nenu pothe povachchunu. His reply has two meanings: (i) " I may possibly go to Moksha" and (ii) If the I goes, one can attain liberation. The second meaning did not occur to any of the scholars. So, taking the first meaning only, all the Pundits felt outraged by the audacity of that uneducated person, who appeared to be totally ignorant of the scriptures and had done no spiritual Sadhana. When the scholars began murmuring among themselves, the king asked that ordinary-looking person, "On what grounds did you make your claim? It appears to be an affront to all the scholars present here". The man politely replied: "Your Excellency! Please forgive me. The meaning of my statement is that if the "I" goes, liberation can be attained. I am sure no one has any objection to this statement of mine". So, the purpose of this story is that the Ahamkara which veils the Buddhi and which leads one to the wrong identification of the body with the Self, should be removed before one can realise the Atma.

The Buddhi is very close to the Atma and therefore well located to receive 90% of the Atmic energy and illumination. The mind derives its power from the Buddhi, the senses from the mind, and the body from the senses. In this process of the flow of power from the Atma to the body in stages, there occurs a gradual quantitative and qualitative diminution of the power. Here is a simple illustration for the quantitative decrease. Suppose there is a dark room which cannot directly receive sunlight. If you want to illuminate that room, you can do it by holding a mirror in the open vicinity and by directing the sun's rays reflected on the mirror towards the interior of the room. However, when compared to the direct rays of the sun, the reflected rays on the mirror are less powerful, and the reflected light in the room is much less powerful. Regarding the gradual deterioration in the quality, let us consider the example of a river. At the source of the springs which give rise to the river, the water will be pure and crystal clear. But as several rivulets and tributaries join its course and as it wends its way through the country side, the river gets more and more polluted as people begin making use of the water. Similarly, the purity of the Atma gets gradually contaminated as it passes through the Buddhi, the mind and the senses and finally reaches the body. Nevertheless, it is possible, through effort, to minimise this quantitative and qualitative deterioration, by sanctifying and purifying the Buddhi and by facilitating the direct influence of the Buddhi on the body.

In the Taithiriya Upanishad which is one of the important among the ten principal upanishads, the Buddhi is described as a bird. "Sraddha" - faith is the head of the bird. Its right wing is "Ritam" - the cosmic rhythm, and its left wing is"Sathyam"-truth. The main body of the bird is "Mahat Tatwa" - the Great Priniciple, its tail is called Yoga. The Buddhi, in its complete form, is thus composed of five constitutents and is extraordinarily powerful.

Once, King Vikramaditya convened an assembly of great scholars and asked them for their opinion regarding which is the most important among the three, viz., Sraddha, Medha and Buddhi. The scholars came out with different answers. However, they finally expressed their consensus that Medha- talent was the most important. Disappointed with their conclusion, the king told the assembly : " Oh Pundits! "Aastha" means Aasakthi or Sraddha - zeal and faith; "Swaastha" means sthiratva and firmness. Without Aasakthi and Sthiratva, Medha - talent is useless. In other words, it would be futile on the part of man to depend only on his talents and cleverness for leading a purposeful life. He should develop faith and zeal together with steadiness and firm determination. Then only will he be able to accomplish great things in his life. Sraddha or faith is of paramount importance. Without Sraddha, you can achieve nothing. If you have a small spark of fire, you can fan it and create a big blazing fire from out of it, provided you have Sraddha. If you lack Sraddha, you will allow even a blazing fire to die out. Similarly with faith, you can produce a mighty banyan tree from a minute seed. Today's man has Sraddha no doubt, but only in securing the fruit and not in the labour required for getting it. He does not have the spirit of work in him. The advances in science and technology have made man a lover of comfort and ease with no interest in hard work. There is nothing wrong with science as such. It is the improper use of science that is leading man astray. What is needed today is to pay attention to love and spiritual advancement along with scientific progress. The difference between science and spirituality is brought out vividly, albeit succinctly, by the two simple equations:

i. Spirit of love = Spirituality
ii. Split of love = Science

When the pleasure -giving objects are transient, and when the body that enjoys the pleasure is also impermanent, how illogical it is to expect permanent happiness from the conveniences and comforts offered by science and technology! If you want permanent happiness, you have to purify you Antahkarana and develop universal love by following the spiritual path.

Today we are witnessing rapid and radical changes in almost every field of life - political, economic, social, scientific, etc. However, there is no mental, ethical and spiritual transformation. This is because no effort is made to understand the nature and role of the human mind. The food consumed by man provides the source of origin, sustenance and development of his mind. After digestion, the grossest part of the food is thrown out as excreta. The subtle part becomes blood and flesh, while the subtlest part assumes the form of the mind. So the nature of the mind depends on the quality and quantity of food consumed. While the gross body or the food sheath - Annamaya Kosa - is chiefly derived from food, the subtle part of the water we drink contributes to the life sheath - Pranamaya Kosa. The grosser part of the water goes out as urine. The food sheath and the life sheath provide the basis for the other three sheaths, namely, the Manomaya Kosa - the mental sheath, the Vijnanamaya Kosa - the intellectual sheath, and the Anandamaya Kosa - the bliss sheath. This shows the paramount importance of food and drink in moulding and developing the human personality.

Reference has been made earlier to the supreme need for ridding the Buddhi of the Ahamkara that often envelopes it. You should understand the difference between Ahamkara

- the ego and the Atma - Self. Atma is the father of Ahamkara, grandfather of the mind or thought, the great grandfather of Vaak - speech. Thus, the Atma, the Ahamkara, the mind-Manas, and Vaak are all members of the same family. Ahamkara is the one that comes and goes, whereas there is no such coming and going for the Atma. Usually, the Sanskrit word "Ahamkara" is translated into English as "Ego'. Both these words are employed in common usage to mean self-esteem or pride born of delusion about one's wealth or scholarship etc. This is a wrong usage of the words. Their correct meaning is the mistaken identification of oneself with the body. All may not be proud of their wealth or knolwedge, but everyone is a victim of Ahamkara in the sense of considering oneself to be the body. It is this Ahamkara that shrouds the Buddhi and misleads it on the wrong path. Hence, if the Buddhi is to develop Sraddha, we should first eliminate Ahamkara.

As mentioned earlier, Ritam, is the right wing of the bird of Buddhi. In vedantic parlance Ritam and Sathyam have been used as synonyms. However, there is a difference between the two. sathyam means putting your words into action, and factually reporting in words what you have done. Ritam, on the other hand, has a wider connotation, namely, purity, harmony and unity of the Trikaranas -thought, word and deed. We may also say that Sathyam is concerned more with the external world, while Ritam relates more to the internal world of mind and its modifications. Sathyam is said to transcend time - past, present and future, while Atma tanscends time and space.

Yoga is the tail of the Buddhi-bird. This tail of Yoga is needed to maintain the required balance between the two wings of Sathyam and Ritam, just as the tail of an aeroplane serves the purpose of balancing the two wings of the aircraft. Yoga as envisaged here should not be confused with asanas, physical exercises of various kinds. Yoga here means the control of the mind and senses.

Then there is the Mahat-Tatwa which is the body of the bird of Buddhi. Mahat-Tatwa signifies the realisation of the Mahavaakya "Tat-Twam-Asi - the great upanishadic declaration : That Thou Art". In other words, it is experienceing one's real Self as Sat-Chit -Ananda. Buddi should not therefore be confused with Medha which refers to the possession of worldy talents, intelligence and cleverness etc., without having Selfknowledge. Thus Buddhi consisting of Sraddha, Sathyam, Ritam, Mahat-Tatwam and Yoga may be considered as the resound, reflection and reaction of the Atma. On the other hand, Medha-Sakthi - the power of wordly knowledge - corresponds to Maya Sakthi - the divine power of delusion.

On Rama's return to Ayodhya after finishing His 14 years of exile in the forests, Kaika, who felt penitent about this grevious wrong she had done to Rama, approached Him when He was alone and prayed, "My dear Rama, Even though I knew about your divine nature, I caused you a lot of unnecessary hardship, blinded by narrow feeling of "I and "mine". Kindly give me some Upadesh - spiritual instruction, so that I may be absolved of the heinous sin I have committed against such a noble person like yourself." In response to her request, Rama did not give her the Upadesh directly, but gave her some hints indirectly. This is characteristic of all Avatars from time immemorial. Avatars seldom give advice directly. Whatever they wish to communicate, they convey more often by way of indirect suggestions and only rarely by the direct method of instruction. The reason for this is there is divinity inherent in every human being, which he can manifest spontaneously, if favourable conditions are provided, just as a viable seed will germinate and grow into a tree because of its inherent nature, if only suitable facilities are provided for the manifestation of its potentiality. Man should be enabled to correct himself by his own efforts, by merely giving timely suggestions, rather than by stultifying his freedom and dignity through directives imposed from without. In short, the best maxim for helping people either in worldy matter or in the spiritual field is : "Help them to help themselves" or "Self-help is the best help".

Following the same strategy, therefore, Sri Rama, in the present instance told, Kaika, "Mother! Please take bath in the holy Sarayu river and come back for My Uapdesh. But while bathing in the Sarayu, please observe what is going along the riverside". Kaika went along with her retinue to the river and returned to Rama after bath. Rama asked her, "Mother! Now tell Me what you noticed on the banks of Sarayu". Kaika replied that she saw a number of sheep and goats gazing the green grass on the banks, bleating "Mae,Mae", as usual, every now and then. Then Rama told her promptly that "Mae, Mae" was His Uapdesh for her. He disclosed to her that the bleating of the sheep and goats meant, "Who am I? Who am I? He further remarked that when even sheep are concerned with the question of , "Who am I?" if a man does not concern himself with this question, he is worse than sheep.

Everyone should first seek to know the answer to the question" "Who am I?" Without knowing who you are, what is the use of trying to know everything about others? At birth you cried out "Koham? - Who am I?" You should not die with the same question on your lips. When you die, you should be able to assert cheerfully - "Soham" -

" I am That or He". Then alone you can justify your birth as a man and enjoy the satisfaction of having fulfilled the purpose of human life. There is only one path to get rid of Ahamkara namely pursuing the Godly way of life. Whenever you feel the sense of ego, sit silently in a corner and observe what your breathing is telling you. It is declaring: "So . . .Ham", - "So" while inhaling and "Ham" while exhaling. The two syllables "So" and "Ham" which together constitute the word Soham convey the meaning : "I am Brahman". If you constantly meditate upon this, your ego-sense characterized by the idea: " I am the body", will cease to bother your. This "Soham" mantra repeats itself in each of you 21,600 times per day. Thus "I am Brahman" is the message of your inner voice all the time. Ignoring this, however, everyone identifies himself with the temporary, artificial name given to the body. Thinking yourself to be Ramaiah, Krishnaiah or Seenaiah - the names given to your body - however long you may engage yourself in spiritual practices, you will not achieve any progress. You will continue to be what you have been according to the name given to your body. "Soham" is the name with which you were born. That alone is your natural and permanent name. That indeed is your Reality or Truth. Realise it and experience Sat-Chit-Ananda. Krishna is known as Partha Sarathi - the charioteer of Partha. Partha does not mean Arjuna alone. It applies to all children of prithvi - the earth. So, make Krishna your charioteer. As the Buddhi is a reflection of the Divine Atma, make use of it as the charioteer in your journey to realise the Atma. Also remember that for success in every endeavour, Prema - Universal love - is essential. The Lord is the embodiment of Love, the Sun of Truth. Therefore, through Love, seek to know your true Self with the help of the Buddhi and purify your mind. This is what I expect of you.

Egoism and Attachment

I am not merit, nor sin.
Neither happiness nor sorrow
Neither mantra nor holy water.
Neither Veda nor Yajna
Neither food nor the enjoyer of food.
I am Sathyam, Sivam, Sundaram - Truth,
Goodnees, Beauty
The embodiment of Sat-Chit-Ananda -
Being -Awarness - Bliss

The above mantra is applicable to everybody. Man is a seeker of happiness, and aspirant for bliss. He strives ceaselessly day and night, to achieve happiness and bliss. In all spheres of his life, he aims at two things: attainment of happiness, and removal of sorrow, What is the inner significance of this perennial quest of man for happiness? Man's very nature is bliss. He is indeed the embodiment of happiness. He is, therefore entitled to seek this birth-right, happiness. If sugar were to lose its sweetness, it ceases to be sugar. If a rose were to lose its fragrance, it would no longer be a rose. Likewise, if a man loses his natural condition of happiness and bliss, he has forfeited his human state. If, for instance, one notices on the road a man with a sorrowful face, he enquires from him the cause for his sorrow. Such enquiry is made by every passer-by, because it is not natural for a human being to be sad. In the same bazaar, however, if some body is going in a happy mood, no special notice is taken of him and no one questions him why he is not unhappy. For, it causes no surprise if a man is happy, because it is his natural condition.

Man has been endowed with the body, the senses, the mind, and the intellect in order to experience his natural state of bliss. But unfortunately, because these faculties or gifts of God are polluted and misused,man is drowned in misery. The body is tainted with the dirt of Raga and Dwesha - attachment and hatred. The senses are shrouded in the soiled cloth of desires and sensuous pleasures. The mind has been polluted by all of these impurities. As a result man is unable to recognise his true nature. He is labouring under the mistaken notion that the worldly pleasures are both dependable and natural to him. In fact, these are all highly transient and ephemeral like the passing clouds.

Recognising that man's moral weaknesses are on the increase, because of the defects in the food that the takes, our forefathers devised simple but sacred ways and means for purifying the food before eating. They used to sprinkle some water on the food, chanting the mantra: "Annam Brahma, Raso Vishnuh, Bhoktaa Maheswarah" - the solid food is Brahma, the drinking water and the liquid essence of the food is Vishnu and the enjoyer of the meal is Maheswara. In performing this purificatory rite, the partaker of food prays to the Trinity to protect him with Satyam and Ritam. The invocation to the deities is to endow him with Trikarana Suddhi - the triple purity of thought, word and deed. By this rite, the food was being sanctified as Prasad. The so-called intellectuals of to-day, puffed up with pride of their talents and skills, are ignoring the efficacy and potency of Sathyam and Ritam.

Sankaracharya during his victorious philosophical pilgrimage through the length and breadth of India, had to engage himself in a debate with a scholarly intellectual by name Mandana Mishra on the subject of "Medha Sakti" -intellectual prowess. Both of them agreed on Ubhaya Bharati to be the umpire to decide who was the winner in the debate.

Ubhaya Bharati was not merely a distinguished scholar but also possessed divine qualities like a pure heart and Buddhi enriched with Satyam, Ritam, Aasakthi or Sraddha, and Stirathwa - stead fastness, cosmic rhythm, zeal or faith, and firmness respectively. Ubhaya Bharati was none other than wife of Mandana mishra. The choice was unique in many respects. It was remarkable that Sankara was willing to have his opponent's wife as the judge. It was the greatest testimony to his faith in the utter impartiality of Ubhaya Bharati, because her Buddhi, endowed with the power of discrimination and objectivity, was superior to the mere intellectual ability which is termed Medhas.

Students must understand that Buddhi is more powerful than Medhas. Buddhi is not mere intellectualism, as commonly understood. It is a peaceful state of the intellect endowed with Aastha or Aasakthi - zeal or faith- and Swastha or Sthiratva -firmness or steadfastness. This Buddhi is the intellect which is enriched by Ritam and Satyam as well as by Yoga and Mahat-tatwa. This Buddhi has not only the power of deliberation and discrimination but also the power of deep insight, enquiry and impartial judgment. Because Ubhaya Bharati had this kind of Buddhi, she declared that Sankaracharya had won the debate. Sankara was extremely pleased with Ubhaya Bharati's unbiased, verdict. Ubhaya Bharati then declared that in accrodance with the understanding between the two contestants before the commencement of the debate, Mandana Mishra, as the vanquished, should take to Sanyasa - monkhood and become a disciple of Sankara. At the same time, as the devoted wife of Mandana Mishra, she decided to become a Sanyasini -nun-herself, in conformity with the ideals of womanhood, according to which the wife should follow the husband in weal and woe.

100

Although she was under no obligation to adopt a monastic life, she did so in order to set an example to the world. After taking Sanyasa, Ubhaya Bharati established an Ashram with the purpose of showing to the arrogant scholars, who relied on mere intellectual acumen or Medhas that it was inferior to Buddhi which is a synthesis of several divine qualities, as mentioned above. One day when she was going to the river for a bath along with her women disciples, she saw an ascetic, who was known for his renunciation of everything in life, sleeping on the wayside, resting his head on a hollow water jug, made of a dried bottlegourd, using it as a pillow and at the same time ensuring that nobody could steal it from him. In order to convey a lesson to the monk, Ubhaya Bharati spoke within his hearing, the following words to her disciples; "Look at that monk who has ostensibly renounced all attachments. Is it not strange that he has not given up his attachment to his worthless water jug"? On hearing these remarks, the ascetic got enraged.He thought," After all she is a woman. Is she entitled to teach me how I should behave?" In a short while when he saw Ubhaya Bharati returning from the river after bath, he flung his water jug at her feet as a proof of his sense of renunciation. Ubhaya Bharati quickly reacted to this, by remarking about him, to her disciples in these words: "Alas! He is not only filled with Abhimana - attachment, but also with Ahamkara -egoism." Immediately the monk ran up to her, fell at her feet regardless of her being a woman, and pleaded for forgiveness of his shortcomings.

From the above episode, it is clear that the root causes of man's bondage are Abhimana or Mamakara - attachment or the possessive sense of "mine" - and Ahamkara - egoism.

Both Ahamkara and Mamakara - attachment and egoism - are the result of consuming improper food. Bad kind of food or food earned by foul means will plunge a man in ignorance in several ways and suppress pure thoughts from arising in him. He will forget what to talk with whom, when, where and how? The following episode in the Mahabharata illustrates this point. Bhishma was a great Jnani - man of wisdom. and also a man of great renunciation - Maha Tyagi. Sri Rama, the hero of Ramayana, is famous for having obeyed his father's orders for only 14 years. But Bhishma followed his father's commandments throughout his life. He got his name "Bhishma", because of his great determination and strict observance of his vows, which are unparalleled in human history. Such a great hero was very grievously wounded by Arjuna's arrows and as a result he fell down on the battle field on the ninth day of the Kurukshetra war.

According to his own grave determination even at that critical period of the fag end of his life, he was lying on a bed of arrows. When the Pandava brothers, along with their spouse, Draupadi approached their grandsire Bhishma to pay their homage to him he began expounding to them all aspects of Dharma from his bed of arrows. After hearing him for a while, Draupadi suddenly burst into laughter. All the Pandava brothers were very much upset by Draupadi's unaccountable levity and considering it as an affront to the venerable Bhishma, they frowned upon her with angry looks. Understanding their distress, Bhishma calmed them down with his soft and sweet words, and told them that Draupadi being an exemplary woman in every respect, must be having a valid reason for her laughter. He then asked Draupadi to explain the reason for her laughter, and thereby remove the misapprehension of her husbands. She replied "Revered grandsire! The lessons of

Dharma which you should have taught to the evil-minded and wicked Kauravas, you are now teaching to my noble and virtuous husbands. This appeared to me both ironical and futile.Hence I could not refrain from laughing, although I knew it would seem impolite".

Bhishma then explained that he had been serving the Kauravas and living on their bounty. He said "As a result of consuming the food received from such ignoble and vicious persons, my blood became polluted and all the pure thoughts in me were thereby suppressed. Now that Arjuna's arrows have drained away all that impure blood from me, the Dharma that was lying buried deep in me, in gushing forth, inducing me to communicate it to your husbands". From this episode, students must realise what a crucial role is played by food in determining one's thoughts, words and actions.

In this connection, it may not be out of place to mention that Draupadi was a "Maha Pativrata" - the doyen among women who worship their husbands as veritable representatives of God and serve them in that spirit moreover there is an esoteric meaning for her name. "Draupadi" does not merely mean the wife of five husbands, namely the Pandavas. Every human being has, within him or her, five husbands in the form of five life-breaths, Prana, Apana, Vyana, Udana and Samana. When it is said that Draupadi lived harmoniously with all her five husbands, the allegorical meaning is that she ensured the maintenance of harmonious equilibrium among her five life-breaths, which is a pre-requisite for a balanced living. In the case of most persons, one or more of these life-breaths become excited beyond the optimum limit, resulting in a loss of equilibrium and harmony among the five life-breaths, and the consequent lack of balance in life as a whole. All should

103

try to follow the example of Draupadi in the matter of leading a life full of contentment and harmony as well as in being satisfied with simple but pure food.

You must realise that food is mainly responsible for your feeling of attachment and hatred - Raga and Dwesha - as well as for Ahamkara and Mamakara - "I" and "Mine". Regulating your food habits is extremely important for the healthy functioning of your mind and intellect. The ways of the mind are really enigmatic. The verdict of the Scriptures is that when man follows the senses he becomes an animal. When he is guided by the mind, he becomes a man. One who acts according to the Buddhi, becomes great among men, while the one who is guided by the Atma becomes Brahman. If you cannot follow the Buddhi, you should at least follow the mind, so that you may at least keep up your human level. But many of you may have the doubt whether the mind itself is not prone to bad tendencies and if so, how to rely on it. The fact is that the mind is pure by itself. It is by implicitly obeying the senses that it becomes impure. Instead of indiscriminately consuming whatever the senses bring to it, if the mind places all such in-take through the senses, before the Buddhi for scrutiny and if it acts according to the decisions of the Buddhi, then the mind will remain unsullied and retain its pristine purity.

Students! Till now, in this Summer Course, we have considered the body, the senses, the mind and the intellect which are all insentient and which together constitute the Kshetra which is also insentient by itself, but which is animated by the Kshetrajna - the knower of the field. The Kshetra and in fact, the entire Srishti - creation, is governed by the three Gunas - Satwa, Rajas and Tamas. Tomorrow we shall discuss in detail about these three Gunas which are remarkably wonderful.

❧

The Three Gunas

Students! Embodiments of Divine Love !

The Divine shines in the rays of the Sun. It is the Divine that reveals to man through his eyes the vastness and glory of the world. The whiteness and coolness of the Moon which confer peace on men are derived from the divine. The universe, which is based on the triple nature of time and which is sustained by the Trinity - Brahma, Vishnu and Maheswara, is permeated by the Divine in the form of the three Gunas - Satva, Rajas and Tamas. In short, everything in the Cosmos is indeed Brahman - Sarvam Khalvidam Brahma.

Nature presents a marvellous picture. No one can fully comprehend it. Whether it is blessing or bereavement, joy or sorrow, gain or loss, it come s from Nature - Prakriti. Nature presides over the destinies of all creatures. This Nature is comprised of the three Gunas. The Trinity represent the three Gunas. The three Gunas account also for the processes of creation, sustenance and dissolution - "Sristhi, Sthithi and Laya". All the varied experiences in the world arise from the three Gunas. Man should aspire not for a long life, but for a divine life. In the Cosmos, which is permeated by the divine, man should seek primarily to divinise or deify his life by transcending the three Gunas.

The secret of creation is known only to the Creator. Others cannot hope to fathom it. Scientists are engaged in exploring the secrets of creation. But none can plumb the depths of Nature's mystery. In scientific investigations, to-day's discovery is superseded by tomorrow's findings. That again becomes obsolete in its turn day-after-tomorrow. Continual change is in the very nature of creation. It is not permanent or immutable. The Creator is the only eternal, unchanging Reality. The spiritual path aims at investigating the nature of the Creator and ultimately becoming one with Him.

The entire Cosmos, consisting of living and inanimate objects, is permeated by the three Gunas. Man should strive to understand the principle that transcends the three Gunas. God is the embodiment of Atma. The terms like Sathyam, Jnanam, Anantam, Brahma, Atma, Bhagavan and God are synonyms.

To start with, the Pancha Bhutas- the five subtle elements of space, air, fire, water and earth emerged from the Atma. each of the five subtle elements is constituted of the three Gunas. Under the influence of these three Gunas, the five subtle elements evolved into the five gross elements and the entire Cosmos, through the process of Pancheekritam-fusion by permutation and combination.

The Cosmos is permeated by the three Gunas - Satva, Rajas and Tamas, At first the nature of creation due to the Satva Guna has to be clearly understood. The Antahkarana - the inner instrument in men represents the total Satvic quality of the five elements. Akasa - space is the first among the five elements. From Akasa emerged what is known as "Suddha Satva" - pure Satva. This accounts for the human form. The Satvic aspect of Akasa accounts also for the emergence of the organ of hearing, the ear. The second element is Air. The skin is the product of the Satvic component of Air. The eye is the organ representing the Satvic principle of the Fire element. The individualised Satvic aspect of the fourth element, Water, is the tongue. The nose represents the individualised Satvic aspect of the fifth element, the Earth. Thus the Satvic components of these five elements account for the five faculties of Sabda - sound, Sparsa -touch, Roopa-sight, Rasa-taste and Gandha-smell. As each of these faculties has emerged from one particular element only, the five faculties are distinct in every person and perform different functions without any overlapping.

Akasa is represented by sound and the corresponding sense organ is the ear. The ear can only hear and not perform any other function. Likewise the skin can only experience the sense of touch associated with Air. The eye which is the organ associated with Fire can only see and do nothing else. The tongue representing the element, Water, can only taste. The nose representing the element Earth can only smell but cannot taste. Thus each sense organ reflects in its functioning, the faculty of the one particular element from which it is evovled.

While each of the sense organs is limited functionally to its specific role, the Antahkarana combines the functions of all the five organs, because it is the cumulative product of all the five elements. This alone has the capacity to experience all the perceptions of the five senses - the five Jnanendriyas. Are these organs of perception functioning externally or internally? The answer is that they perform a dual role - both internal and external. If only the physical organ, the ear, is present, but if the faculty of hearing is absent, the ear cannot hear. If the faculty of hearing is present, but there is no ear to receive sounds from the outside world, the faculty is of no use. It is the combined operation of the Jnanendriyas - externally organs of perception and the corresponding invisible internal sense -centres in the brain that accounts for the functioning of the human personality. For example, if you want your voice to reach a vast audience, you should have the mike inside and the loudspeaker outside. Loudspeaker without mike or vice versa cannot serve the purpose.

While the combined operation of the five elements in their Satvic aspect is seen in the Antahkarana, the collective functioning of the five elements in their Rajasic aspect expresses itself as the life-force -Prana. Among the five elements, in their individual expression of their Rajasic quality. Akasa is represented by the Vaak - voice. Vayu finds expression in the hand. Agni expresses itself in its individualised Rajoguna as the foot. The fourth and fifth elements - Water and Earth find Rajasic expression in the two excretory organs in the body.

In this context, you must take note of some significant facts in the functioning of these elements. In its Satvic aspect, Akasa expresses itself as ear. But the same Akasa, in it Rajasic aspect appears as the Vaak -faculty of speech. It may be inferred from this that Akasa has two children the ear representing Satva and the Voice representing Rajas. The ear, which is Akasa's first child, receives the sounds coming from outside. The second child, namely voice, sends its reaction from the inside to the outside, in the form of words. Likewise the skin is the first child of Vayu in its Satvic aspect. The second child, in its Rajasic aspect, is the hand. For instance, the skin recognises an ant crawling on the body. Immediately the hand tries to remove it. It will be seen from these examples that the Satvic quality is concerned with receiving impressions from outside, while the Rajasic quality is concerned with casting them out by way of reaction. In other words, the Jnanendriyas orginating from Satva receive stimuli from outside and the Karmendriyas derived from Rajas respond to the stiumli.

In the world to-day what is happening is the exact opposite. What is Rajasic is being taken in and what is Satvic is being rejected. In the natural scheme of creation, what should be received is that which is Satvic and what should be rejected is all that is Rajasic.

The primary quality of Nature - Prakriti - is Satva. Prakriti is called "Stri" made up of the three syllables - Sa, Ta and Ra. The significance of this term is : first of all, you have to take in what is Satvic, secondly "Ta" implies developing some Tamasic qualities, like submission, humility and modesty. "Ra", representing the Rajoguna, implies that there are occasions in life when some firm resolutions and stern actions will have to be taken. The Rajasic quality comes last and it means that Rajasic actions have to be done as a last resort when they are unavoidable.

In the cosmic process, it is the Satvic quality - the 'Sa' kara or the syllable "Sa" that comes first. Hence the duty of every one to develop the Satvic quality in every aspect - in thoughts, attitudes, words and deeds.

The next aspect to be understood is that under the influence of Tamoguna, the five subtle elements evolve themselves into the five gross elements by the process of "Pancheekritam" - fusion through permutation and combination. This highly complicated process may be illustrated by the following example for purposes of easy understanding. Suppose the five elements come together as five individuals each having a one rupee coin. Now, each of them exchanges his one rupee coin for one half-a-rupee coin and four two-anna coins. A two-anna coin is equivalent to one-eight of a rupee. Then, Akasa retains half-a-rupee and distributes among the other four elements one-eighth of a rupee each. The second element Vayu also does likewise retains half-a-rupee for itself. Fire, Water and Earth also follow the same procedure. As a result of this redistribution, each has one rupee, but its composition is affected by the exchanges among the elements, of parts of their respective nature. Originally each element was whole by itself. The process of mixing has resulted in the presence of all five elements in every "rupee". This means that ultimately each element is composed of half of its original nature, the second half consisting of one-eighth of each of the other four elements. For example, the composition of Earth will be 1/2 Earth +1/8th space +1/8th Air +1/8th Fire +1/8th Water. Similar will be the composition of the other four elements. In relation to the human being, the process of Pancheekrita makes man a mixture of the five elements and creates diversity from unity.These have been described in spiritual parlance as Shodasa Kalas - the sixteen aspects. What were these sixteen aspects? They are, the five Jnanendriyas - organs of perception, the five Karmendriyas - organs of action, the five elements, and the mind. Every man has these sixteen constituents, although the sixteen kalas are attributed only to the Divine. The implication is that man has to realise his divinity.

To-day man's desire for worldy pleasures has exceeded all limits, and what is more, he wants quick fulfilment of his innumerable desires, by resorting to short-cuts. But he must realise that short cuts are always dangerous and riddled with thorns, stones etc. The highway is always preferable, though it may seem longer. The ways of the Divine are not easy to comprehend. Wishing the welfare of everyone in the universe, the Divine uses a myriad methods. It may be illustrated by the story of a devotee, aspiring for riches, who performed a severe penance for securing a boon from the Goddess of Wealth, Lakshmi. Man is prepared to undergo any ordeal for achieving material wealth, but will not take any trouble to realise the Divine. Lakshmi appeared before the devotee and asked him what he wanted. He replied that he wanted Lakshmi Herself. She agreed and said that adorning Herself with all ornaments, She would follow him and asked him to go ahead. She said she would come to his house and hand over all her ornaments to him. She imposed, however, one stipulation. "You must go ahead of me and never look back. If you look back, I will stay back at the spot". Filled with joy, the devotee strode ahead towards his home. The Goddess's jewels were making all kinds of sounds as She walked behind. Unable to restrain his curiosity to find out what were all the jewels she was wearing, he turned back to have a look at her. He could not repress his desire till he reached home. The moment he looked back, Lakshmi stopped there and did not follow him. This is what happens when one cannot contorl one's desire. Even though he got the grace of the Divine, the devotee could not benefit from it. This means that even if you are blessed with an abundance of Divine grace, you must acquire the capacity to benefit from it. To get this capacity, you have to obey implicitly the injunctions of the Divine. If the devotee in the story had adhered to Lakshmi's conditions, he would have benefited from her bounty. Failing to abide by her conditions, he forfeited what he had been offered.

The situation in the world is something similar to this. The world is permeated by the potency of the three Gunas. Even our vision of the world is influenced by the three Gunas. Examine your eye. The outer rim of the eye is red, representing the Rajo-guna. After that, you have the white area, representing Satva. At the centre is the black circular cornea, representing the Tamo-guna. Thus even our vision is tainted by the three colours, red, white and black representing the three Gunas.

111

When you pose the question, "Where is God"? the answer is given by nature herself. The revolution of the Earth on its own axis at the speed of 1000 miles per hour accounts for the phenomenon of night and day. The earth's rotation round the Sun at a speed of 66,000 miles an hour accounts for the various seasons, for rainfall and the cultivation of food crops. Thus the divinely -ordained motions of the earth enable living beings to get their food. This is a visible proof of the existence of God. The Scriptures declare that the foolish person, even while seeing the acts of God, declares he has not seen God. He does not realise that Nature is the vesture of God. What is the lesson to be learnt from the observance of Nature? It is "Kriyaseelata" - being always active in the performance of one's duty. It is because Nature ceaselessly performs its duty that the world is able to derive so many benefits.

The secret and mystery of creation lies in the due performance of one's duty with earnestnesss and sincerity. In the pursuit of the mirage of sensual happiness, men are going on the wrong path. This can be seen in the life-style of people going to work, or carrying on business. After what they consider as a day of hard work, they go to clubs, where they become slaves of drink and ultimately ruin themselves, because :

> *First the man drinks the wine,*
> *Second the wine drinks the wine,*
> *Third the wine drinks the man.*

Real happiness can be got only be rendering service to the public. Go to the help of the poor and the forlorn. You will derive strength as well as peace form such service. Your conscience also will feel satisfied. It is a pity that neither the rich among the public nor the administrators are inclined to do such service. It is all the more essential

112

that students should have some ideals before them and look forward to serving society selflessly. You should realise that you are a part of society and that your welfare is bound up with the good of the society as a whole. You should utilize your knowledge and skill for the benefit of society, duly recognising the fact that "Knowledge without action is useless, and action without knowledge is foolish".

Whatever Sadhana you may or may not do, your primary concern must be to develop the love of God. When you develop that pure love, you can achieve anything.

In this context, the advice which Hanuman gave to Vibhishana when the latter lamented that though he had been chanting the name of Rama since long, he had not had the benefit of a vision of Rama, is relevant. Hanuman told Vibhishana that it was not enough to merely chant the name. One should also engage himself in the service of the Divine. Hanuman declared that while meditating on the name of Rama, he was also engaged in constant service to the Lord. That was how he had earned Rama's grace and become near and dear to Him.

On another occasion, Vibhishana complained to Hanuman, saying , "My dear friend, I am in the midst of cruel Rakshasas - demons just like the soft tongue which is surrounded by the sharp teeth. Hence I am unable to calmly concentrate on Rama". Hanuman promptly replied, "My dear Vibhishana! Do not be worried on that account. In old age, the teeth fall away but the tongue remains in tact. Likewise the demons will be destroyed in due course like the teeth, and you will remain safe like the tongue. So be happy."

That is why Vibhishana used to praise Hanuman as Gunavantha - highly virtuous, Balavantha - extremely strong and powerful, and Saantha - always calm and peaceful.

Remember that like Hanuman, you too can derive strength and peace only through love and service, together with control of the senses. The young student Prahalada told his father, Hiranyakasipu, "You have conquered all the worlds in a trice, but you are unable to control your senses. How can you call yourself a ruler, when you are yourself ruled by your senses?" So, students should strive to control their senses, and develop love of God, fear of sin, and morality in society.

Know Thyself

O Gudakesa ! - Conqueror of sleep, Arjuna!
I am the Atma residing in all beings.
I am also the beginning, the middle and
the end of all beings.

Gita (ch. X, verse. 20)

Embodiments of Divine Love!

In the above verse of Gita, Krishna tells Arjuna, "I am the Atma - the Self-residing in all beings; I am also the beginning, the middle and the end of all beings". That is to say that the entire Cosmos consisting of moving and non-moving objects is only the Atma. Nothing exists other than the Atma or the Self. What to-day's man needs to do is to constantly contemplate on the Self, to realise the Self, to be firmly established in the Self and to experience the bliss of the Self.

Atma is also known as "Awareness". It is this awareness that is responsible for the "I" consciousness in all beings, which is called "Aham".When this Aham identifies itself with the body, it becomes Ahamkara. This is the false "I", and not the real "I". What hides the Atma always, is the mind. The clouds which are formed due to the Sun's heat hide the Sun itself. Likewise the mind which is the off-spring of the Atma hides the Atma itself. As long as the mind is there, man cannot hope to understand anything about the Self, not to speak of realising and experiencing the bliss of the Self. That state in which one is established in the Self at all times and under all circumstances is called "Sakshatkara" - Self-realisation.

The first sound that emanated from the Self is "I". The entire creation began only after the emanation of this

115

"I" sound. If there is no"I", there is no creation. The terms "I", Brahman, Atma or Self are all synonymous. The "I" sans mind is the Atma or the Self in its pristine purity. The "I" associated with the mind is the false self or Mithyatma. There is only one Atma or Self and that is the "I".

The paradox, however, is that to experience his own Reality - what he already is- man is undertaking several Sadhanas or spiritual practices. All such practices undertaken for seeking the Self are activities in which man engages himself during the state of Ajnana - ignorance only. You will not find the Jnani - the realised one - doing such Sadhana, because for him, there is no distinction such as the means and the end. If man is practising Sadhana, it is merely for his mental satisfaction. Such practices which are pursued for mental satisfaction will only serve the purpose of strengthening the mind instead of destroying it, as recommended in the teaching s of Vedanta. If at all you want to do Sadhana, the only right approach to it, is the dispel the "Anatmabhava" - the false notion of the "non-self". If, instead of doing this right thing, you go on worshipping three million Gods and Goddesses, disregarding the common truth taught by all the Scriptures of the world that there is only one God, or if you pursue all sorts of so-called Sadhanas to attain Self-realisation and liberation, what does it indicate other than your mental aberrations, hallucinations and delusions?

It is important to recognise that as long as the mind is there, desires will not leave you. As long as you have desires, the false notion of "I" and "Mine" will not leave you. As long as the feeling of "I" and "mine" is there, Ahamkara - your wrong identification with the body - will not leave you. As long as Ahamkara does not leave you, Ajnana -

ignorance too will not leave you. In effect, it means that there is no way other than the annihilation of the mind to attain Atma-Jnana-knowledge of the Self, or Atma-darshan-vision of the Self, or Atmananda - Bliss of the Self, whatever you may choose to call it.

The mind, the Buddhi or intellect, the Chitta or memory, and ahamkara or the ego sense - what is the substratum from which these four have emerged, by which they are sustained, and into which they will merge back? That substratum is the "Brahman"; that is the "Atma" or the Self. So, instead of recognising the source of your origin and your own identity, what is the use of your trying to attain it by taking recourse to other pathways? It looks as ridiculous as a theif putting on a Police-man's dress in an effort to catch the culprit i.e. himself!

What is the need for all other Sadhanas, in order to recognise yourself? There is a small story in this connection. Once a party consisting of ten fools happened to cross a river. After fording the river, one of them wanted to verify whether all the ten of them had reached the bank safely. He counted all the others, forgetting himself, and began weeping, telling them that one member of the group was lost in the river. The other fools in turn also did the same mistake by repeating the counting in a similar manner. As a result they all began making a hue and cry. In the meanwhile, a passer -by who noticed their miserable plight approached them and asked them the reason for their piteous lamentation. When they told him that one of the ten members of their group was washed away in the river while crossing, the passer-by understood their ignorance and asked them to stand in a row. Then he counted them aloud one by one, thereby convincing them that all the ten of them were intact, and that their wrong conclusion about the loss of one man was due to the face that everybody forgot himself while counting.

One who has forgotten himself cannot recognise the truth proper. When you are yourself the Atma, how can you recognise it by praying to some other being or doing such other Sadhana? Because the "One has become many" = "Ekoham bahusyam", you have developed a liking for the diversity, forgetting the unity. All these things that you see around you are your own reflections, as if in a mirror. Leaving the actual object, you are running after the reflected images. Your own bhrama - delusion is binding you hand and foot. One who is bound by bhrama cannot reach Brahman - God. All your Sadhanas are futile, if you want to experience the Self. All these Sadhanas will only serve the purpose of quietening the mind. The quietened mind may again become agitated. What is important is to get rid of the mind, by understanding its true nature.

The right kinds of Sadhana for seeking the Atma are only those that are directed toward the destruction of the mind. Because of his identification with his body, man is being helplessly tossed hither and thither in various ways by his ego. "I am doing this; I am enjoying that; I have conquered this" thus saying to himself, man is lending strength day by day, to his sense of doership - Kartritvabhava. Students! remember that success and failure do not depend on your efforts or Sadhana and such other activities. You are simply inflating your ego - "Ahamkara", by deluding yourself that you have been able to achieve things by your own effort. Look around and see the many instances where the best of efforts have not been crowned with success, while with little or no effort victory has come unsought in the case of many others. Instead of getting frustrated due to failures by depending on your

118

efforts have not been crowned with success. While with little or no effort only, you can surely win success by dedicating all your activities to the Divine, by considering them as the Lord's work, and by undertaking them with unwavering faith in God. You should have the firm conviction that nothing happens due to human effort. Proof for this assertion need not be sought for in some far-off place. It can be found right within your own body. For instance, what effort are you making of for the ceaseless beating of your heart or for the incessant breathing of your lungs? Does the digestion of the food eaten by you take place, because of your will? Are you able to live because you want to live, or die because you want to die? Does your birth take place according to when and where you desire? If you ponder deeply along these lines of thought, you will discover that your feelings of "I" and "mine" -Ahamakara and Mamakara - are being unduly fostered by your false sense of doership and enjoyership -Kartritva and Bhoktritva.

To-day we are preoccupied with various activities just for our mental satisfaction. But the mind never knows any satisfaction, whatever we may do and for how long. Mind alone is Maya - illusion. Mind alone is desire. Mind itself is Avidya - ignorance. Mind alone is Nature - Pakriti. And mind alone is delusion - Bhranti or bhrama, Deeply immersed in this Bhrama, how can you hope to attain Brahman, without getting rid of your Bhrama? Seeing your own shadow, you are trembling with fear! You are afraid of your own feelings and imaginations! However, "Reality is one" - "Ekam Sat". And that is "Atma". Scholars describe God as the embodiment of Sat, Chit and Anandam - Existence -Awareness -Bliss. It is not correct. He is Sat itself, He is Chit itself, He is Ananda itself. These three are not different or separate from God.

"There is some mighty power, unknown to me, different from me and far away from me", - thinking thus, some people resort to meditation. "There is some secret and sacred divine power distinctly separate from me and I must acquire it" - imagining thus, some others observe many vows, perform several rites and undertake various austerities. All this is sheer ignorance. As long as you think there is anything different from you, so long are you submerged in ignorance. There is nothing in the universe other than you, or higher than you. To think otherwise or to try to prove otherwise is nothing but your "Manobhranti" - mental delusion, resembling a dream. In your dream you see many sights and experience various things, but for how long are they real? Only as long as your dream lasts. When the dream ends, they are all unreal. Similarly, your hardships, losses, worry and sorrow etc are real, only as long as your mind is under delusion. Once the delusion leaves you, they will all be unreal. They will then turn out to be castles of myths created by your mind.Relying on the false "I", You are rejecting the real "I". You are boosting your Ahamkara by thinking continually that you are the body.

If only we can understand one small but subtle truth, we can expand the horizons of our thoughts and feelings to any extent. There is nothing other than the Self in the universe. All the things you see as existing in the phenomenal world are but reflections of the One Self. In the case of mundane affairs, the subject, the object and the predicate - all these three are present. But in spiritual matters relating to the Atma or Self, there is only the subject, but no separate object or predicate. In fact, all these three aspects get merged into one Atma-tatwa - the priniciple of the Self which pervades everywhere as Chaitanya - consciousness. There is no place where consciousness does not exist. This very Chaitanya has been partitioned, so to say, into three aspect s of Sat, Chit, Ananda for the satisfaction and understanding of the laity. These three aspects have been described by the Vedantins as mutual reflections of one another. They have used the terms Asthi, Bhathi and Priyam for Sat, Chit and Ananda respectively. But all these three refer to one and the same entity. For example, here is a tumbler. It exists - hence it is Sat. When it is seen by us, it creates in us an awareness that it is a tumbler - so, it is Chit. We are making use of it - therefore it is Ananda. But the tumbler has not become three; it is only one in which all the three aspects are united. This illustrates the unity in diversity relating to the Self. The Self is formless, but appears in different forms. Let us consider the example of air. It is formless, but we cannot deny its existence, just because it has no form of its own. Actually it assumes the form of the container that is used to hold it - the form of a ballon, or foot-ball, or air-pillow. Althought the Self has no form, it has the quality of Chaitanya consciousness.

It is difficult to understand the nature of this priniciple of consciousness. There are three aspects of this consciousness, depending upon its association with specific aspects of the human personality. When this consciousness or awareness is associated with the senses, we use the term "conscious". When it is associated with the mind, we call it "conscience", and when it is associated with the Self, it is pure consciousness. These three terms are being used in daily parlance for convenience, just as we call one doctor as heart specialist, another doctor, as E. N. T. specialist, and so on. But all of them are doctors. Likewise all men are embodiments of one and the same Self, although they may be engaged in different occupations like agriculture, business, government service, labour etc. As long as you have the body, the senses and the mind etc., it is very difficult to experience the unity of the Self. But just because it is difficult, you should not give up or relax your effort to experience it, because it is worth much more than all your effort.

We have till now understood the human body as the Chariot, the senses as the horses, the mind as the reins, and the Buddhi as the charioteer. But we should recognise that all these are only meant to serve the master- the Atma or Self. Our wakeful state represents Rajoguna - the state of activity; the deep-sleep state symbolizes Tamoguna-the state of inertia; and the transition between the waking and sleeping states represents the Satva guna - the State of equilibrium and equipoise which is of the nature of the Self. You have to understand what Self-knowledge is to appreciate the nature of the Self. We shall discuss the subject of Atma-Jnana or Self-knowledge tomorrow.

Self-knowledge

Dear Students!

God is more taintless than the sky. The Sun, the Moon and the stars are His eyes. He is all-pervading like the air. It is only when we thoroughly recognise the nature of the Upadhis or vestures of man like the body, the senses, the mind and the Buddhi, that we can understand the sacred, pure and infinite Atma or the Divine Principle.

Know Me as the Kshetrajna - Knower of the Fields - in all Kshetras - Fields;

The knowledge of the Kshetra and Kshetrajna is alone true knowledge, in My view".

(Gita, Ch.13, Verse 2)

The whole world is a combination of Kshetras and Kshetrajna - the Fields and the knower of the Fields. The Kshetra of the human body is but a reflection of Prakriti - Nature. All the sentient and insentient aspects of the universe are in the human body. The entire universe is a reflection of the inner being of man. It will not suffice to know about the body, the senses, the mind and the intellect only. There is a s distinct Kshetrajna who animates all the Kshetras. If you understand the Kshetrajna, there is no need to know about the Kshetra; but till then you should pay the required attention to the Kshetra. To understand the Kshetrajna, you need a special kind of knowledge. Book knowledge, superficial knowledge, general knowledge, discriminative knowledge, experience - knowledge, practical knowledge - all these pertain to inert matter and mundane things and have an individual bias. All these kinds of knowledge will not help in understanding the Self. You need a diamond to cut another

123

diamond. You need a thorn to remove another thorn that has pierced your foot. Toexperience the Self-Atma, you require only Self-Knowledge, Atma -Janana. Today what we regard as knowledge - Jnana - in this physical world is nothing but ignorance - Ajnana. Self-knowledge alone is true knowledge. In fact, whether you call it "Atma" - Self or Jnana - knowledge -they are both one and the same. True awareness is Jnana. Jnana, Jneyam and Jnanam - the knowing, the known and the knower. - predicate, object and subject respectively - such triads are not applicable to this Atma-Jnana or Self-knowledge.

These triads and such other classifications pertain to the level of the mind, whereas Self-knowledge reveals itself after the annihilation of the mind. The still and peaceful silence that follows the destruction of the mind is itself true knowledge. This true knowledge is our very nature, and not something to be newly acquired. However, this knowledge is hidden by the mind and its aberrations, like the cinder covered by the ash, generated by the cinder itself, like the water shrouded by the moss produced by water itself and like the eye covered by the cataract arising from the eye itself. Remove the cataract and you get back your sight. Remover the mind and the self-knowledge stands revealed automatically.

This knowledge can neither be obtained from books, nor given by gurus - the spiritual teachers nor can it be conferred as a boon by the Paramatma - the Supreme Soul. Indeed you are yourself Paramatma, Atma or Jnana. Sitting in solitude, when you calmly enquire how this Jnana is present in all, you will hear from within yourself a sponteneous voice that is eternal and changeless. All the things in this manifested world are subject to constant change due to the process of union and seperation of atoms, that goes on endlessly. However,this divine voice within is not only the same in all beings, not only eternal but also it remains unchanged by anything The changes due to the change in the age of a person, or due to the changing states of consciousness like waking, dreaming and sleeping, affect only the gross, subtle and causal bodies, but they do not, in any way, affect the voice referred to above. What then is that voice? it is the divine inner voice emanating from the Atma as I, I, I - Aham, Aham, Aham. It is this Aham that is the source of Soham mantra that goes on repeating itself, without any conscious effort, in all of us during the process of breathing. It is this Aham again that appears as Ahamkara when it identifies itself with the body. Ahamkara is human; Aham is divine. This Aham can be realised only by purifying one's heart, never by studying scriptures and becoming a scholar.

You see the phenomenal universe, only as long as you have not crossed the thereshould of the mind. Once you go beyond the mind, you will experience nothing but the Self. On reaching the sea, the river loses its individuality, its name and form and becomes one with the sea. So also the knower of Brahman verily becomes Brahman.

When there is a pot, and also water in the pot, you will see the reflected image of the sun in the pot, but even when all these are absent, the Sun is ever present. Similarly , even when the reflecting media of the body - the pot, -the mind and - the water - are not present, the Self will always be present, although one may not be able to see the Self or even its reflection. A note-worthy point, in this connection, is that the image of the Atma that you get through the media of the body and mind is not true to the original Atma. It is similar to the reflecion of your face in water, wherein your left eye appears as your right eye and vice versa. So also, when you are travelling in a train,

125

your sight deceives you by giving you the impression that the trees and mountains etc outside are in motion., These two examples serve to illustrate the point that all the distinctions you see in the phenomenal world are due to the distortions of your mind only. You have to go beyond the ,mind to realise the eternal truth.

People believe that every man has a free will. It is an entirely wrong belief. They imagine that it is because of man's will, determination, Sadhana and effort that he is able to achieve success. This is all due to the aberrations of their Ahamkara and the reflection of their false sense of doership. Take the case of Karna, the hero of the Kurukshetra war in Mahabharata. He had all the where-withall needed for victory, mighty weapons, great physical and intellectual prowess, dauntless courage etc. etc. But with all his resources and assets, he suffered a crushing defeat and humiliating death in the battle field. Why? Because he lacked only one thing, namely, the grace, help and support of the Divine. So, even for attaining success in the matter of attaining Self-knowledge, it is foolish to rely on one's physical, mental and intellectual abilities and resources. What is needed is to recognise and cultivate the spirit of oneness of all that exists.

It is an undisputed fact that to-day a number of modern facilities, conveniences and gadgets like aeroplanes, auto-mobiles, cinemas, television sets, computers, radios and videos etc are available in plenty. However,d the basic and pertinent question that should be asked in this connection is : "Who is the beneficiary of all these amenities?" No doubt, the answer to this quesion will be"I". If only the "I" is there to start with, all the rest will follow. In the absence of this "I" there is no producer and no consumer; hence no need to produce. Thus it can be seen that everything centres around the "I". In other words, "Men are more valuable than all the wealth of the world:. However, it is important to recognise that, man is essentially divine. And this divinity cannot be experienced except through Atma Jnana - Self-knowledge.

Bhakti is the best means to experience this Atma-Jnana and enjoy Atmananda - the bliss of the Self. What is Bhakti? It is constant contemplation on the Self. Bhakti and Jnana are not two different things. Bhakti itself is Jnana. And Jnana itself is Bhakti. They are closly inter-related and inter-dependent. The singular bond that unites Bhakti and Jnana is Prema -Divine Love. With this sacred cord of Prema, you can bind the Lord Himself.

The Bhagavd Gita exhorts: "Uddareth Atmanaa Atmaanam" - "Elevate yourself by your own efforts". Contrary to this exhortation, there are many persons labouring under the wrong notion that if they beget sons, the latter will help them to reach heaven after their death, by performing the Sraaddha ceremoeny. It is foolish to think that those having sons reach the higher worlds and those having no sons will go down to the nether worlds. Further, Sraaddha does not mean inviting the Brahmin preist, washing his feet, feeding him sumptuously and obtaining his blessings. The real meaning of Sraaddha is to offer Pinda with Sraddha or faith at the Lotus Feet of the Lord. And what is Pinds? Pinda is not the rice ball as usually understood but the human body. Therefore, the true Pinda-dana is to offer your body, all your physical and mental faculties and skills in the service of the Lord who has manifested Himself as the universe.

In Vedantic parlance, the human body is also called "Tunga-bhadra". "Tunga" means very high, vast, great etc. "Bhadra" means good, sacred, auspicious, effulgent etc. The implication of calling the human body as "Tunga-bhadra" is that it is intended to undertake such noble activities as will bring about the welfare of the society. Therefore, to be worthy of this name, you should dedicate your body and mind to the loving service of all beings. In this context, you must remember the shining example of the great musician - Saint, Thyagaraja who proved himself worthy of his name which literally means - the e"King of renunciation". When he ruler of Tanjavur sent him a number of precious jewels and provisions necessary to run a house-hold, he refused to accept them and sang extempore, addressing his mind thus: " Oh my dear mind! What is it that gives real happiness, wealth or the Lotus Feet of the Lord? Please tell me the truth". Then he also sang a prayer to the Lord as follows: "Oh my beloved Lord Rama! Do you want to tempt me with these riches, and make it an excuse for deserting me? I have held fast your Lotus Feet with both my hands. How can these hands now leave your sacred feet, which are my permanent and precious treasure, in order to receive this transient tinsel of tempting wealth?' Therefore, just like Thyagaraja who proved himself worthy of his name, you should also prove yourself worthy of the name "Tunga-Bhadra" which the scriptures have given to the human body.

Students! This Summer Course is a golden opportunity for you. So many elderly and eminent persons with rich experience behind them are giving you very valuable information. You should, however, utilise all this information for your transformation, which is possible only when you put into actual practice at least a few things out of the many things you have been hearing.

What is Freedom

How glittering and quivering is the
waterdrop on the lotus leaf!
So is man's life in this transient world;
Life is rife with strife, disease and delusions.
Alas! Sorrow and suffering reign
supreme in this sordid world
Therefore, O foolish mind! Take refuge
In the Name of Lord - Govinda, Govinda, Govinda!

Dear Students!

People in general cannot understand what is Aadhyaatmikam or spirituality and what is individual freedom. Spirituality does not mean living in solitude, far away from the society. On the other hand, true spirituality consists in sowing the seeds of love in the hearts of all people and facilitating the blossoming of peace and divine love among all mankind. If you enquire deeply into the nature of the divine principle, there are not two things like spirituality and individual freedom.

If one is allowed to express one's feelings and thoughts from a public platform without any let or hindrance, it is said to be freedom for the individual. But the truth is that no one has absolute freedom in this universe. The word freedom has been used freely and frequently in the political field. What is freedom? To get rid of foreign rule and to establish the rule of the natives of the nation was considered as freedom before India got her political independence. But that was neither individual freedom nor fundamental freedom. It was only a replacement of foreign rule by indigenous rule, with little or no change in the aspect of freedom as such. After the departure of the foreigners, we thought that the natives got their freedom. But in what aspect did we get freedom? What is the use of simply repeating 'freedom', 'freedom'. It is only when we have achieved unity that we can claim to have attained freedom. Without achieving unity, if we talk of freedom, it is merely the freedom of words but not the freedom of the individuals. True freedom springs forth from the level of the Heart.

What is meant by the Heart? Not the physical heart full of flesh and blood. The real Heart is that which has no connection with any particular place, time, individual or country. It is the Divine priniciple which is equally present in all persons at all times, in all places and in all countries. This Heart has no form. What we consider as the heart inside the human body comes in the middle and goes in the middle. But what we call as Heart in the spiritual parlance knows no coming or going. It is eternal and changeless. Therefore, true freedom consists in recognising and realising this Heart or Divine Principle, knowing which one becomes the knower of everything.

"Yatha Andande tatha Brahmande".As is the microcosm, so is the macrocosm. Microcosm refers to the individual and macrocosm to the aggregate or sum total. One who knows his Self knows all. To-day's man tries to know everything about the world. He feels proud that the knows everything. But he forgets that he does not know himself. Mention is made in one of the Upanishads of a great sage by name Uddalaka who sent his son Svetaketu to another Guru for his education. Svetaketu took twelve years to acquire proficiency in all the branches of learning. Puffed up with pride, he returned to his father and told him about his profound scholarship. Then the father questioned him, "Oh my son! have you known that by knowing which you would be knowing everything." The son was baffled by this question which gave a shattering blow to his pride of learning. Of all the kinds of pride, the pride of learning is the worst. By putting that question which intrigued his son, Sage Uddalaka made him recognise the superiority of Self-knowledge or Atma Jnanam as compared to Loka Jnanam or secular knowledge.

When you ask one, "Who are you"? and if he replies, "I dont' know who I am", what will you think of him? You will consider him to be a mad fellow. Similarly, if you try to know about everything else without knowing who you are, are you any better than that mad fellow? Therefore, first of all, you should try to know who you are. You may say, "I am Ramaiah", But Ramaiah is the name given to your body. But who is that "I " in your reply, who is separate from Ramaiah? You should understand the nature of that "I". That "I" is nothing other than the "Hridayam" or the Heart. That "I" is the Atma or Self. That "I" is Brahman or the Supreme Reality. This Heart is all-pervasive or Omnipresent.

Consider this illustration : A painter has painted a beautiful picture of a dancing girl on a sheet of paper. The picture shows her body and limbs with several bends and curves, ups and downs in the process of dancing. In another painting, there are high mountains and low valleys. But if you feel the paper by touching with your fingers, you will not find actually any ups and downs or elevations and depressions in both the paintings. So also, in the phenomenal world, you find many differences like ups and downs, good and bad, sins and virtues, truth and untruth, pain and pleasure etc. But at the level of the Heart, you will not at all find these dualities or pairs of opposites.

Let us consider another example. Here is a tumbler. It has a name and a form. If you remove or ignore the name and form, what ramains? Only silver. It was silver

131

before becoming a tumbler. When it has the form of a tumbler also, it is only silver. If the tumbler is destroyed and made into a round mass, it will continue to be silver only . So it is nothing but silver in the beginning, the middle and the end. The name and form of tumbler were there only in the middle, but neither in the beginning nor at the end. That which does not exist in the beginning and the end, but exists only in the middle is considered to be really non-existent even in the middle also. Its apparent existence in the middle is only a myth or illusion. That is why the phenomenal world is called Mithya jagath - illusory universe.

Ekam Sath - Existence is One. When there is no second, how can the question of freedom or bondage arise? So these concepts of freedom and bondage are the concoctions of your own mind. We give attention and value to the moon, only when there is no sun. Why do we give value to the moon, when there is no sun? The moon has no effulgence of its own. It shines only due to the reflection of the sun's rays. Similarly, when we do not see the sun of Self, we give value to the moon of the mind. The Vedas have revealed that the mind is a reflection of the moon. Therefore we cherish the mind and nourish it by devoting more and more time and attention to it, as long as we do not engage ourselves in Atma vichara or Self-enquiry. It is only when you have the mind, that you see all such differences as spiritual and secular, sacred and mundane, freedom and bondage, man and woman, Prakriti and Paratatwam, Nature and Absolute Reality. All the dualitites are the creations of the mind.

I wish to clarify some points relating to the debate that took place here on the subject of freedom and bondage. Suppose there is a man suffering from dire poverty. He is very hungry. Even in spite of begging, no one gives him food. Then he feels that he has the freedom to resort to stealing, in order to appease his hunger. Although he may rationalise thus, because of his selfishness, his conscience does not approve his stealing. So how can it be called freedom, when it is disapproved by his conscience? It may, at best, be called freedom with bondage. When does one have real freedom? Only when the mind is destroyed. When you use words "Swabhava" and "swechcha", you have to understand their true meaning. "swa" means Self or Atma. Hence "Swabhava" means the nature of Atma. Likewise, Swa+ichcha= "Swechcha" which means the volition of the Atma. Strictly speaking, it should be understood as volition which is in line with the Atma, since Atma *perse* has no volition. In the light of these meanings, it is incorrect to use the terms "Swabhava" and "Swechcha" in connection with matters relating to the activities of the body, senses, mind and intellect. It should be recognised that man's life is regulated by the laws of Nature on the one hand, and by the man-made rules and regulations on the other. Such being the case, there is no validity in everyone thinking for himself that he has freedom to act as he likes. It is only God that may be said to have freedom. Even this is a relative truth, because in absolute terms, Existence is only one, and hence the word "freedom" is out of place in this context.

People talk glibly about surrender. Some persons complain, "I have completely surendered myself to Swami, but there is no end to my problems, hardships, suffering and sorrow". In My view, this is no surrender at all. True surrender never takes into congnizance the presence or absence of sorrow, suffering or misery and the like. There are some others who say, "When I sit in meditation,

I sometime go into Samadhi". But what is Samadhi? In books written by worldly people with mundane views, one may find various descriptions of Samadhi. While in meditation, a person may lose body-consciousness. But this cannot rightly be called Samadhi. It may be a symptom of weakness, fits, hysteria or emotion, but never a sign of Samadhi. Merging the mind in the Atma is alone Samadhi. In that state, one does not see or experience duality. Samadhi = sama+ dhi, which essentially means equal-mindedness. In that condition, there will be no trace of such differences like pleasure and pain, gain and loss, virtue and sin or "Prakriti and Paramatma - Nature and God". This alone is the evidence of equal-mindedness. This truly is "Swabhava" - nature of the Self. In contrast to this, if a man aspires for something in his life and pursues various paths to achieve it, you may take it all as an indication of mental aberrations.

As long as the mind is there, no one can claim to be enjoying freedom. In the wordly parlance, one may say, "I have money. I am giving it to him. This is my freedom etc". But truly speaking, this is neither freedom nor free will . The mind is a mixture of the three Gunas - Satva, Raja and Tamas. One or more of these three may become dominant at a given time in a given person. In the present instance, the mind of the man who is giving some money to another person is motivated by the Satva-Guna to give something in charity to the needy person. Hence, when a man acts under the influence of the Gunas, how can he claim to have freedom of will? It is therefore, impossible for any body who is a part of the creation to have freedom. Justice Khastagir told you, little while ago, that a person has freedom to take exercise by waving a stick as he likes in the compound of his house; but he has no such freedom to do so in a public road, because it is against governmental

134

rules and regulations, and he is liable to be arrested by the Police. However, strictly speaking, where the man takes exercise by waving his stick in the premises of his residence, what is involved is not freedom but only the fulfilment of his wish or desire. Whenever a man does something for the sake of his personal benefit, it only signifies his desire for that thing. That alone can be termed as true freedom which emanates from the Heart, irrespective of the place, time, person or thing.

The highly talented persons in different walks of life have not acquired their skills from somewhere outside. All these are but manifestations of their own innate potentialites. It is sheer ignorance to think that any person can be developed by some other person. Fverything is in you alone. All that you do by way of your effort is to manifest or give an outer expression to what is already inherent in you. So, even in the spiritual field, all the Sadhana that you need to do is to remove the obstruction, namely, the ignorance that is preventing the manifestation of the divinity already present in you. Krishna too taught this very truth to Arjuna as follows :

"Arjuna, you did not know the art and science of archery when you were born. You are under the impression that Drona instructed you and therefore you acquired the skills of warfare from somewhere outside. It is not correct to think that Drona taught you and that you learnt these skills afresh. All that Drona did was to facilitate the manifestation of what was already in you. Remember that any teacher or even any great man endowed with extra-ordinary powers cannot bring out what is not already inside you. Luck or ill-luck, bliss or misery - all these are in you only. Suppose you are digging a well. On reaching the depth of, say, 100 feet from the

135

ground-level, you strike a good spring with copious supply of water. Now, have you created the water or brought it from somewhere? No, no; water was there all the while. It came to view because the earth that was hiding it was removed. So too, there is divinity ever present in you. But you have forgotten it. Why did you forget? Because of your wrong identification with your body.

As long as there is mind, man cannot escape from thoughts of various kinds. These indicate the freedom of the mind, but not freedom of the man. Sampath has told you that a student has the freedom to question the teacher and obtain answers. But this does not come under "freedom". It comes under duty; the duty of a student is to abide by the regulations of the educational system which provides for asking questions and obtaining answers. You should understand the difference between freedom and duty. Duty may be considered under three categories: "Sambandham -relationship, Nirbandham - compulsion and Kartavyam - obligation. The differences between these three will be clear if we consider some examples.

You wanted to give a tea-party to your friends on a Sunday evening. Accordingly, you invited your friends in advance. But at 4. p. m. on Sunday you developed high temperature. So you informed all the invitees that the tea-party is postponed. In this situation, you may or may not have the tea-party, as you wish. But this is not freedom; it is "Sambandham - relationship", something voluntary and optional.

Next, about "Nirbandham", You are in the office. Suddenly you are attacked by high fever. On that very day, your director or boss is coming to inspect your office. So you cannot go on leave of absence. Therefore, you run to the doctor, take an injection and some tablets for your illness and attend office compulsorily in spite of your suffering from fever. This is a case of "Nirbandham" or compulsion.

Thirdly "Kartavyam". Due to some reasons there arises a quarrel between you and your wife. In a fit of anger you beat your wife. She goes away into the bed room and lies down, weeping in agony. She does not attend to cooking. You are sitting in the drawing room. You are extremely angry on two accounts - firstly for the reason which led to your quarrel and secondly because your wife has not cooked food and you are very hungry. So due to the combination of both anger and hunger, you are very restless. Just then, a good friend of yours comes to visit you. You greet him with a smile, saying "Hallo, Hallo" and after offering him a seat, you go inside and tell your wife in a hushed voice but with an angry tone "My friend has come, prepare coffee". You show an angry face to your wife but a happy countenance to your friend. You don't want your friend to know that you are angry with your wife, nor do you want your wife to know that you are jolly with your friend. Since you are thus obliged to adjust your behaviour to suit different persons and situations, in conformity with the social norms and etiquette, it is called Kartavyam or obligation.

Now-a-days people in general, have given the go-by to all the three - Sambandham, Nirbandham and Kartavyam - relationship, compulsion and obligation. Hence there is "Dharmaglani" - an all round decline of righteousness in the modern society. It should be noted that there is no freedom for man in acting according to "relationship, compulsion and obligation" as illustrated above. There is freedom only at the level of the Atma or Self.

Engage yourself in any activity, but always keep in view your true nature as the Self or Atma. If you do so, you will surely enjoy real freedom. There are not two kinds of freedom - individual and spiritual. "Adhyatmikam or spirituality alone is "Swaatantryam" or freedom. Freedom alone is spirituality. It is not possible for these two to exist separately. There is only one entity which has assumed different names and forms. Just as the same milk assumes the different names and forms of curd or yoghurt, butter-milk, cream, butter etc. Similarly Saalokyam, Saameepyam, Saaroopyam and Saayujyam are different names for the same spiritual experience. These four, however, are progressive steps in the process of God-realisation. ":Saalokyam means always thinking of God and living in the spiritual world or God's world. so to say, as against the material world. "Saameepyam" indicates moving closer to Swami or God. 'Saaroopyam" means becoming one like Swami. "Saayujyam" is the final stage of becoming Swami Himself. i.e., complete merger without any trace of duality.

If any one in this phenomenal world says he is having freedom, we can call it only "verri Swaatantryam" or crazy freedom. It may also be called "Ahamkaara Swaatantryam" i.e . freedom of the ego,. and "Abhimaana Swaatantrayam", i. e., freedom of infatuation or attachment. It is foolish on your part if you think you have the freedom to scold and beat your wife or children. If you want to enhance your freedom by suprressing the freedom of others, it is utter selfishness only. True freedom lies in not interfering with the freedom of others. You do not find such freedom in this world. What you find in this world is a hierarchy of controls, the one at a higher level controlling the one at a lower level. This results in lack of freedom for all except perhaps for the one top-most person in the hierarchy. But strictly speaking, even this one person occupying the top most rung of the hierarchical ladder cannot be said to have freedom, because the question of freedom does not arise when there is only one without a second. What we call "individual freedom" and "fundamental rights' may serve the purpose of enabling us to carry on our mundane affairs. But in the absolute sense, there is no true freedom involved in these matters.

From the above discussion, we arrive at the conclusion that, from whatever angle we may consider the matter, there is no freedom for man and there can be no freedom for man. In fact, man does not know what true freedom means. One who has freedom does not take birth in this world. One who enters the world with a body, cannot have freedom. Jayamma gave you the example of an animal tied to a peg or stake with a rope of ten feet length to illustrate that the animal has a limited freedom within a diameter of ten feet. But how can you speak of freedom when the animal is tied by a rope to the stake at one end and to its neck at the other end, and when it cannot go beyond ten feet? Anything that is bound by any limitation whatsoever, cannot and should not be said to have freedom. This only shows that we are in the habit of using words without knowing their correct meaning.

If you understand the true meaning of the "Heart", you will recognise that it is beyond all limitations. The same Heart that is within you is also within all others including even those who are hated by you or who hate you. You may have the doubt that if all have the same Heart, why should their thoughts, attitudes and actions be different. Students! Remember that all these differences are created by the mind and they have nothing to do with

139

the Heart. This is not the physical heart but the spiritual Heart which is omnipresent. It has no form but it is the substratum for all forms, just as sugar is the common basis for all kinds of sugar dolls of different animals which are liked by different children.

All the differences you find in the world are only reflections of your mind. Whether you love some one, or hate some one, or ridicule somebody, they are all your reflections only. If you give up these "reactions, resounds and reflections" of your mind, which appear to you in the phenomenal world, and get hold of the Heart called Reality, then all these differences in thoughts, feelings, actions etc. would disappear. God does not have thoughts and feelings of any kind. But He appears to respond suitably according to the thoughts, feelings, attitudes, and actions like worship, prayer etc. of the devotees. He has no likes and dislikes. Nor is He angry with some and pleased with some others. He does not have moods that change from time to time in respect of the same person or different persons, as is imagined by many of you. Of course, as a result of putting on a body, the Avatars also appear to have such reactions, resounds and reflections but it is only to set an example to others and to help them to reform themselves, so that they may make the needed progress in their spiritual journey. God does not differentiate or discriminate between "high" caste and "low" caste, between the young and the old, between men and women, between people of one country and another etc. etc. These are all mundane differences pertaining to the phenomenal world but have nothing to do with Divinity. It is only narrow-mindedness to think that Rama was born in a Kshatriya family, Krishna in the

Yadava or cowherd family, or Sai Baba in Raju-Kshatriya family and so on.

God will never have such differences. If one understands rightly the nature of the divine principle of the Atma, there will be no scope for such petty, narrow-minded differences and discriminations.

Living in this vast universe, you must develop broad thoughts and feelings, to understand the nature of the infinite Atma. Spirituality should not be approached from a narrow standpoint. Doing worship, Bhajans or devotional singing, meditation and the like are considered by many as signs of spirituality. But all these are only mental aberrations, and serve to give only mental satisfaction to the practitioners. You praise God, saying, "Lord, you are my mother, my father, my friend" and so on. But why all this mumbo-jumbo or gibbberish? Why not simply say,"You are I. I am you" and be done with it? In this connection, it is not correct to say, "You and I are one", because you and I are we, but never one. It is better to say, "We and we are one", because I am in you and you are in Me. Therefore, when we come together, we become one. However in the statement: "We and we are one", there is duality, because the "we" consists of the physical body and the divine principle of the Atma. If you understand the nature of these two aspects of your personality, you will not think of the relationships like mother, father, friend etc. between yourself and God. You are both one, although you may appear as two. Here is a concrete illustration for this. The mike in front of Me appears as two, but functions as one only in the process of amplifying my voice so as to make it audible to all of you. Similarly you should visualise and realise the unity of the body and the

Hridayam or Atma. This is the one sadhana you should practice.

Students! Spritiuality means merger with God. You are not different from God. You are God, God is you. If you are firmly established in this faith, you need not undertake any other Sadhana or spiritual practices. Of course, some people repeat parrot-like, "I and you are one", but they do not live up to it. Here is a small story to illustrate this. A Guru gave the mantra "Sivo-ham" to one of his disciples and told him that the mantra means "I am Siva". As the disciple was uttering, "Sivo-ham, Sivo-ham". a friend of his came and asked him about the meaning of the mantra. On being told about the meaning of the mantra, the friend questioned him, "If you are Siva, how is Parvati related to you?, The immediate response of the disciple was: "May God forgive my offence! Goddess Paarvati is far superior to me and deserves my adoration and worship." The point to be noted here is that if the disciple had real faith and conviction in the mantra, "Sivo-ham" which implies that there is only one God who appears to have assumed all the names and forms of all gods and goddesses, as well as of all beings in the entire universe, then the correct answer to his friend's question would have been, " I am Parvati too". Instead of that this wrong reply was due to his belief in the traditional husband-wife realionship - that Parvati was Siva's consort. Therefore, this kind of complications will arise if you think of God in terms of such worldly, physical relationships like mother, father etc. Instead of that you should have unshakeable faith in the unity of Godhead and assert, I am you, you are I; we are not two, but one". This is the true freedom inherent in you. In this context you should understand the correct meaning of the terms "Swadharma" and "Paradharma" used in the Gita. The meaning of "Swadharma" is Atma-dharma, and not the dharma or duties enjoined on the different castes like Brahmana dharma, Kshatriya dharma and so on. Likewise, "Paradharma"means "Deha-dharma" - dharma pertaining to the body. It is in this sense that you should understand the declaration in the Gita: "Paradharmo bhayavahah", which in effect, means that if you follow the "deha-dharma" or the dharma of the physical body, fear will be your lot in life. On the other hand, if you follow the "Atma-dharma", there will be no fear for you. If you thus understand the real meanings of the verses and words in the Gita and if you mould your lives accordingly, you will have no fear of calumny, ridicule, sorrow and suffering.

Students! You may or may not believe Me, when I say, "I do not know what sorrow is, what worry is, or what hardship means! Some may praise Me and worship Me. Others may criticise and vilify Me. It is their will and pleasure in either case. I am not at all bothered. My attitude towards others abusing Me is: if they abuse or scold Me aloud, I say, "Gone with the wind", if they abuse Me silently within themselves, I say, it hurts them only, for, it does not reach me." In either case, why should I be worried at all? Therefore, if you are established in Truth, you will never be affected by praise or blame, by joy or sorrow. People come to Me and complain about the bereavements in their family or some suffering or pain etc. I respond to them by saying "Chaala santosham", which means " Very happy". You should note that this kind of happiness remains the same under all circumstances, because it is based on the "Atmatatwa" - that is, "Everything is Atma". However, sometimes I pretend to be angry with the students, because of their wrong behaviour. But it is

143

only outward anger, it does not come from inside. I may not speak to some persons for months together. That is the medicine to cure them of their disease of misbehaviour, and to set them right. What right has anybody to ask why Swami is not talking to him?

A small example for this. Four patients come to a doctor. They have all come with the same complaint of stomach ache. The doctor examines them one after the other. He sends away one of them with the advice to have hot water fomentation. For the second patient he gives a mixture of mag sulph and soda bicarb and tells him that he will be relieved of his stomach ache which is due to gas trouble. For the third person, he gives some tablets. But he wants the fourth person to undergo a surgical operation immediatley, because his stomach pain is due to appendicitis. Similarly, I give different treatments to different persons based on their needs and for their own good. I don't look at all at some people. I don't speak to some. I avoid or by pass some people although they try to attract my attention. These are all my prescriptions for their respective diseases. Why do I administer such medicines or treatments? I have got principles. My word is very precious. Even if you don't give value to My word, I attach great importance and value to My word. If somebody does not heed My word, I dont' like to waste My words by speaking to him. Hence in order to save the value of My words, I stop talking to such persons. Instead of complaining that Swami does not talk to me, why don't you blame yourself for not acting according to Swami's instructions? This is not "One-way traffic". It is a matter of "give and take" . If Swami 's orders are implicitly obeyed by you, His Grace is showered on you automatically. You need not specially pray for His Grace.

First of all, attach value to your own words. Remember the wise saying, "Truth is the life of a word; a battalion of brave soldiers is the life of a fort; modesty is the life of a woman, and signature is the life of a promisory note or bond".

All cannot understand the nature of Divinity. God is never elated or depressed. Even if the whole world blames and reviles Me, I will not be depressed. Even if the entire world extols Me, I will not be elated. This is because I am established in Truth. There will be no room for any worry or anxiety if you are firmly established in the Heart or Atma or Truth, - all of which mean the same. Try to understand the divinity of Swami, who is the changeless support or Adhara of all that changes - Adheya, and thus sanctify and justify your stay here for this summer course.

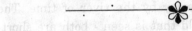

Practice and Precept

Dear Students!

The world in which we live is impermanent. Youth comes in the middle and goes in the middle. It is not a sign of the educated to gloat over their impetuous and turbulent youth. As for wealth, it is as momentary as the lightning. Wife and children join you midstream and leave you midstream in the river of life. Before marriage, who was the wife and who was the husband? So also, before birth, who was the mother and who was the child? Wife, children and other relatives are like the travellers who meet and depart over night from a caravansarai. All these are transient. What then is permanent? Only two things: Dharma-Righteousness and Keerthi-Fame. As the scriptures have declared: "Yat drisyam tat nasyam" - whatever is visible is perishable. The entire manifested universe will be washed away by the river of time. The eye that sees and the world that is seen - both are short-lived.

Without developing the Jnana-Chakshu - the eye of wisdom, if a man is content with the Charma Chakshu - the physical eye only, he is no better than the birds and beasts. Human life is invaluable, purposeful and worth experiencing and enjoying. For the fulfilment of such a precious and sacred human life, the acquisition of Atma Jnana-Self-knowledge is highly indispensable. The scriptures proclaim, on the one hand, that among all beings in the animal kingdom, it is a rare privilege to be born as a human being. They also declare on the other hand, that a man devoid of Jnana is equal to a brute. The physical eyes of man can see only the gross external world but not the inner divinity which is highly subtle.

As a matter of fact, the physical eyes cannot even see all the gross things; for example, the eyes cannot see themselves without the aid of a mirror; they cannot see some parts of the very body to which they belong, for example the head and the back. So, when these physical eyes are incapable of seeing even the entire gross body to which they belong, how can they see the subtle mind? When they cannot see even the subtle mind, how can they see the Atma which is the subtlest of all? Therefore, the physical eyes are helpful to man, only for carrying his mundane activities in the phenomenal world.

The eye of wisdom is highly essential to every man. Jnana-Netram - the eye of wisdom. Divya-Netram - the divine eye, Atam -Netram - the eye of the Self, Brahma -Netram - the eye of Brahman - all these names are synonymous. Only when you have the firm faith that all is Brahman - Sarvam Brahman, you will see the entire universe as Brahman. That is why the scriptures have exhorted; Fill your vision-Dhristi, with Jnana -wisdom, and you will see the Srishti - creation, filled with Brahman - The Supreme Absolute. The colour of the entire prakriti - Nature, depends upon the colour of the glasses through which the physical eyes look at it.

All things that are visible are subject to change. However, the substratum of all this changing phenomena is the changeless Divine Principle - Brahman, just as the stationary road supports the movement of the fast running buses and cars. Only if you recognise the changeless Divine Principle that supports the changing universe, can you easily understand the entire secret of the universe. Your mind is the cause of your inability to understand the real nature of this world. The characteristic of the mind is Pravritthi - external orientation. Man is wasting his life, night and day, for acquiring external things like houses, lands, vehicles, wealth and other so-called "properties" which, in fact, are not "proper ties". Is it for the sake of these trifles that man is born? No. No. No. To realise God is his foremost task in life. Man must realise God, feel God, see God and talk to God. This is realisation. This is religion. It serves no purpose if one knows everything else but does not know God.

A few minutes earlier, Anil Kumar spoke to you about botany. The flowers and fruits which we want from the tree and which are seen on the tree top depend on the unseen roots below the ground for their growth and development. So, in order to get a good harvest of flowers and fruits, we need to apply water and manure not to the visible flowers and fruits, but to the invisible roots which alone can give them nourishment. Likewise it is the Divine Principle - Atma Tatwa that serves as the root for the tree of this world. It is mentioned in the Gita that God is the seed of all beings. What is the significance of this statement? When you plant a seed in the soil, it germinates and in due course of time it grows into a big tree with several branches. Each branch puts forth many flowers which develop into so many fruits. Each of these fruits will have a seed in it similar to the seed that gave rise to the tree. Thus from one seed, you have got hundreds of seeds of the same type.

Now, according to the Gita, God is the seed that has given rise to the tree of this vast universe. Each country is a branch of this tree. In each branch there are a number of fruits, namely, various kinds of living beings, each of which carries within it the seed of Divinity. It means that in every being, God is there in the form of the spirit or Atma. Students of to-day are not making

148

any effort to recognise this subtle truth behind the gross universe. They spend all their time for specialising in one of the subjects like Physics, Chemistry, Zoology, Botany, Mathematics, Commerce etc. so that they may earn their livelihood, never giving any thought to the goal of life, which is more important than making a living.

According to one of the most important mantras in the Veda, immortality can be obtained only by Tyaga-renunciation but not by good actions, progeny or wealth etc. But what exactly is renunciation? It does not mean giving up one's wife and children, or house and other properties. What actually is your bondage? It is the delusion of your identification with the body. You must give up the false idea that you are the body and imbibe the truth that you are the Atma. Then alone can you achieve liberation - Moksham. Deha-virakthi - detachment from the body consciousness will free you from the grief of bondage and Daiva Aasakthi-attachment of God will give you the bliss of Moksha - liberation and merger with God. How to get rid of Deha-bhraanthi-body-consciousness? Not by giving up food and drink, reducing the body to a skeleton and courting death, but by asserting with faith that "I am not the body. The body, the senses, the mind and the intellect are all my instruments-Upadhis". You must give up your body-consciousness, just as you remove your soiled clothes.

In the debate that took place the day-before-yesterday, it was argued that one has the freedom to eat when hungry and drink water when thirsty. But how can you call this freedom? You are forced to eat food to appease your hunger and drink water to quench your thirst. Here you are simply following the law of Nature. There is no question of freedom in this. It is only bliss that is connected with freedom. How can you have that

149

bliss? Can you get it from the body or the mind? Not at all. The bliss that you may derive through the body and mind is but momentary. You have not been born just for this kind of transient and trivial joys. You have yourself put on this human body to enjoy ever-lasting bliss.

All things happen according to the Divine will - Daiva Sankalpam. By your own effort you cannot achieve anything. The day-before-yesterday, I told you how in several instances, men could not achieve things in spite of all their efforts, and how success came seeking those who had not tried for it. It is only due to Ahamkara that you wrongly appropriate to yourself both doership and enjoyership - Kartritwa and Bhoktritwa. You are the very embodiment of bliss. Bliss is your very nature. But it is a tragedy that you are unable to recognise it and experience it. This bliss is veiled by likes and dislikes, the sense of 'I' and 'Mine', hesitation and doubt, pleasure and displeasure etc. Raaga and Dwesha - attachment and hatred, are the thick clothes which shroud the bliss in you. When you get rid of attachment and hatred you can discover your own real nature. How strange and foolish it is that despite yourself being the very embodiment of bliss, you are searching for bliss elsewhere! Although everything is within you, you are unfortunately running after petty desires and silly sensual pleasures in the phenomenal world. What is the reason for this mad race? Ignorance of the truth that you are yourself the source of all bliss.

Students! You know that the gigantic elephant with a giant's strength meekly submits to the control of the puny driver holding the spur. Why? Because the elephant is ignorant of its own strength. Similarly the black bumble bee can burrow holes into a very hard wooden beam, and go in and out of it. But the same bee enters into a

150

tender and soft lotus flower, gets entrapped and dies, because it knows not its own strength. Likewise, man does not try to recognise his innate divinity, sacredness and bliss. Leave alone his failure to try; what is still worse, he refuses to believe even when told about it. Students! If you put forth the required effort, you will definitely experience the truth of your own divinity and bliss. The musk-deer, not knowing that the musky fragrance emanates from its own navel, roams about restlessly all over the forest, in search of the source of that smell. At last it becomes very tired and lies down in the shade of a tree for taking rest. While lying down, it keeps its nose near its navel, and then recognises that the fragrance is coming out of its own navel. And now it says to itself, "Alas! what a great fool am I! Not knowing that I myself am the source of the fragrance, I was searching in vain all through the forest, putting myself to unnecessary trouble!" This is the nature of ignorance. This exactly is the plight of man too. Nityanandam - eternal Bliss, Brahmanandam - infinite Bliss, and Advaitanandam - non-dual bliss are the very nature and form of man. But lured by the momentary sensuous worldly pleasures, man is unable to seek, to understand and to enjoy this supreme divine bliss. Unlike the so-called bliss derived from material things, the bliss of the Atma is never tainted by sorrow. If you fill up a vessel with Payasam - a sweet made by boiling a cereal in milk with sugar and then you make several holes in the vessel, what come out of any or all of these holes will be only the sweet Payasam. Similar is the case with Atmananda - the bliss of the Atma, which manifests itself in various ways. That is why the sages have named the Atma as Ananda and described it variously as eternal bliss, supreme bliss, absolute bliss, bliss of wisdom, bliss transcending all the pairs of opposites, pure bliss, unshakeable bliss, bliss that is beyond the grasp of the mind, bliss which transcends the three Gunas and so on. When such priceless treasure of bliss is readily available within you, why should you foolishly run after this phenomenal world which brings you trials and tribulations, sufferings and sorrow?

The treasuries and banks which contain huge sums of money are provided with the required safety and security measures - strong iron gates, steel chests and huge locks, besides night and day watch by fully-armed watchmen. Likewise the invaluable treasury of bliss is being constantly guarded by the highly poisonous serpent called Ahamkara. But what is the cause of this Ahamkara? Is it wealth, strength, position, power or learning? No, none of these. The root cause of Ahamkara is Deha-bhranti - mistaken identification of oneself with his body. As for the other things like wealth, position, power etc., it must be clear to you that all the past history and the present happenings in the world as well as the teachings of the Gita and scriptures, reveal that all these are highly transient. They do not follow you even up to the grave, not to speak of beyond the grave. What accompanies you even after death is the good or the bad done by you during your life-time.

Students! Don't forget that "as you sow, so you reap". This is the inviolable Law of Karma, in which Indians have firm belief. Before entering into action, ask yourself thus: "I am the embodiment of the divine Atma, is it proper for me to engage myself in this mean, despicable action?" If you practise such self-restraint and self-discipline, you will be able to keep yourself away from evil, and move closer and closer to the Atma. Make use of your talents and resources for the welfare of the world rather than for making quick money by resorting to treachery and corruption in pursuit of self-interest.

Patriotism - love for the land of one's birth - is extremely important. Once when Subhas Chandra Bose was a student of the Calcutta University, a British Lecturer spoke disparagingly about India and Indians. Young Subhas Chandra was upset by this, but restrained himself from retaliation for quite some time. However, when he found the Lecturer exceeding the limits of decency and decorum, he could not contain himself any longer. He sprang to his feet, swiftly jumped across the benches and pouncing upon the Lecturer, thrashed him with his shoe. In a few minutes the news spread like wild fire throughout the University Campus. The authorities held an emergency meeting and passed orders debarring Subhas from the University for a period of five years. Thus Subhas sacrificed his education for the sake of upholding the honour of his motherland. Consequently his father sent Subhas to London for his higher studies. There, too, Subhas evinced his sense of patriotism. He had distinguished himself in his studies there and hence he had good opportunities to stay back in London, had he been interested in his self-advancement. But prodded by his patriotic fervour, Subhas returned to India after passing I.C.S. - Indian Civil Services examination with a high rank and entered politics instead of Government service. Therefore, students should follow his example and sacrifice their 'Swartha' - selfish interest, for Paraartha - the welfare of others, and attain Paramaartha - the supreme goal of life.

Remember that Bhagavad Gita, Bible, Koran, Granth Sahib and other holy scriptures are not intended for 'Paaraayana' - mere recitation. They are meant for

153

Aacharana - practice. It is not a sign of Bhakti - devotion, if one memorises all the 700 verses or the Gita or give learned commentaries thereon. It is only a proof of ostentation.

To-day what the world needs are men of action - Aachara Manavaas, and not men of words in human form - Aakara Manavaas. By your intellectual acumen, you may aspire for such titles of honour like Padma Sri and Padma Bhushan, but you cannot hope to win the title of Amrita Putra - children of immortality - the title which the Veda proclaims as the birth-right of man. There can be no other title equal to, or higher than this title of Amrita Putra. And it is for this title that you must all strive. You should develop Desabhimanam, Daivabhimanam and Dharmabhimanam - love of country, love of God and love of Dharma. There is no Dharma higher than Sathya, and no Sathya higher than Dharma. Sathya and Dharma are inseparable and inter-dependent. Try to practise them to some extent atleast, and spread the benefits to the society at large. Then only you will understand what bliss is. Bliss is the goal for which you undertake any activity - mundane or spiritual. Bliss is the goal of all religions. The paths may be many but the goal is one just as jewels are many, but gold is one, and cows are many, but milk is one. Therefore you should never criticise any religion. Along with your education, try to develop equal-mindedness, and universal love, so that you can experience the unity in diversity.

Ascent of Man

It is God's greatness, grandeur and majesty
that you see in the sky-scraping peaks
of the high mountains;

It is His sublime silence and His supreme
peace that you find in the remote forests and
the vast deserts;

It is His glorious effulgence and beautiful
splendour that you witness in the sun, the moon,
and the countless galaxies in the sky;

It is His love and creativity that you find
reflected in the inhabitants of villages, towns
and cities that adorn the earth.

Whatever thing of beauty you come across in this
universe is a reminder of, and a tribute to the
"Source of All Beauty" - the Divine Lord!

Mallamma of Karnataka State gave simple but charming description of God's omnipresent beauty in the following words: "Lotus flower is the ornament for the lake. Houses are the ornaments for a village. Waves are the ornaments for the ocean. Moon is the ornament for the sky". Whatever things of beauty you see in the world are but the reflections of the one source of all beauty - the Divine Lord. That is why the Upanishads have described God as Sathyam, Sivam and Sundaram - Truth, Goodness and Beauty. The ornament for mankind is "Maanavatvam". This "Maanavataam" is indispensable for human society. Whether one is a reputed scholar, an eminent scientist, or a great administrator, the development of human qualities is most essential for every-one.

155

The development of the society, the state and the nation is proportionate to the development of Maanavatam or the Human state. If human qualities are lost, the honour of the society and the nation will be lost.

The honour of mankind depends on its morality and integrity. It is essential for the students of to-day to foster the human qualities. The human values can progress and thrive only in a spiritual environment. It is only when seeds are sown in the soil and watered regularly that they will sprout and develop into big trees which yield good fruits. Instead of this, if the seeds are kept in a tin and watered, they will only rot and perish. Likewise, morality and integrity can thrive only in the human heart. Morality is the fulfilment of character and conduct. Morality elevates man to a higher level. Since time immemorial, India has been sharing her spiritual wealth with the other nations of the world and spreading among them the message of morality and integrity. Morality and integrity alone are the real and eternal temples of God. In the absence of morality, the human race will go to rack and ruin. To-day, the supreme need of this country and the world is morality. It is extremely necessary to observe morality in all places and in all situations. Marshal Pope taught that morality should not be violated even in times of war or any crisis including risk to one's life. William Gladstone, Prime Minister to Queen Victoria strained every nerve to safe guard morality at all times and therefore, people respected him more than even the queen.

Morality is achieved through the control of the senses. He alone can control others, who can control himself. How can one who has no self-discipline enforce discipline on others? Only when there is harmony between one's words and actions, can a man achieve great things in his life.

"If a man practises what he preaches,
He is not an ordinary man, but a Mahatma - greatman.
If a man says one thing and does another thing,
He is only a beast, not a man".

In the modern society, there is no concord between words and deeds. If there is harmony between one's words and action, it is Sathyam. If there is harmony between one's thought, word and deed, it is Ritam.

To-day's students do not know what is sense-control. This is called Samyama - self-restraint. Only man is capable of this Samyama. Man is forfeiting his divinity by giving a free reign to his senses. The control of sense organs is called Damam in Sanskrit. One who has achieved Damam is called a Daanta. What we need in to-day's world are Daantulu - people with control over their sense organs, but not Vedaantulu - people well versed in Vedanta. To-day Vedanta is confined to oratory and ostentation; the practising of Vedanta is on the decline. No wonder, therefore, that there is scarcity of Ananda or bliss.

Every student should become a Daanta. Even before acquiring knowledge, to-day's student is becoming saturated with egoism, pride and ostentation and is running amuck in society. Students are not even aware of discipline and obedience. They do not know how to talk, and behave with elders. Of course, the students are not to be blamed entirely for this state of affairs. The parents and the teachers are neither setting a proper example to them, nor encouraging them in such matters. That is why the condition of students is deteriorating day by day. Students should try to behave properly, to control their senses, and thereby to foster peace in society. The youth of to-day are fond of frivolous talk. This has

157

become a hobby for them. They are allergic to good and gentle words. Spirituality is a matter of ridicule for them. Such deplorably bad atmosphere among the students is ever on the increase, so much so they are not in a position to understand even the purpose of education. They should, first of all, disabuse their minds of the wrong notion that the purpose of education is for securing jobs and earning money. They should not forget the fact that education is intended to help them to reach the goal of life. Of course, they need to take up some jobs for earning their livelihood. But they should scrupulously adhere to morality and integrity in performing their duties, without stooping to indulge in immoral practices like corruption and cheating etc. Knowledge and money are not bad in themselves. Goodness or badness depends upon how you make use of them.

Students! The air that we inhale has to be exhaled. Otherwise the lungs will be damaged. Likewise, the knowledge you learn and money you earn should be used for the good of the society. Otherwise they are as worthless as the dust under your feet. You should repay your debt to the society which has contributed to your education and earnings. This is real Seva or Service. This kind of spirit of sacrifice is conspicious by its absence among the present-day students. Earning and hoarding - this sort of one-way traffic seems to be their ideal in life! Many of you know how to swim. You must be aware that unless you push back the water, you cannot move forward in the process of swimming. This shows that without sacrifice, you cannot achieve progress in life. You have to sacrifice not only your money, but also your bad qualities. Giving up bad qualities is the true sacrifice or renunciation. Renouncing your wife and children, or wealth and property is not a great sacrifice.

It is easier than giving up your evil propensities. And the latter alone will lead to the full blossoming of the human personality.

Students! To live as a true human being is the great task of man. It is a blot on the human state for a man to live like an animal. The humanness in man is being crushed to extinction by the Arishadvarga - the gang of the six internal foes, namely, Kama, Krodha, Lobha, Moha, Mada and Matsarya - desire, anger, greed, delusion, pride and jealousy. The moon can shed her cool, bright light on the earth in full measure, only when she has developed all her sixteen kalaas - attributes in full. Man, on the other hand, can shed his effulgence on the society, only when he gets rid of the sixteen bad qualities, namely the six internal enemies Arishadvarga - eight kinds of Mada - pride, and the two qualities of Rajas - restlessness and Tamas - inertia. He must also give Kartrithva and Bhoktrithva - the sense of doership and enjoyership. With the faith that all is Brahman - Sarvam Brahman if one engages himself in good actions and dedicates them to the Divine, one will receive God's grace and the help needed by him. Potana, the great devotee and poet who wrote the Telugu Bhagavatam dedicated his work to Lord Rama at the outset, by saying that Rama was the real writer and he (Potana) was a mere instrument in Rama's hands. There is a great spiritual significance in Potana's verse of dedication, which is a re-statement of the famous Mahavakya, viz, "Tat-Twam-Asi - that-thou-Art. In the present instance, Tat or That is represented by the Divine Lord Rama, Twam or Thou by the poet - devotee Potana, and Asi or Art by the book Bhagavatam. In other words, Bhagavan, Bhakta and Bhagavata - God , the devotee and the scripture are three in one. Moreover, the five letters "Bha-ga-va-ta-mu" have their own spiritual significance. These five letters may be considered as the five elements, five senses, five sheaths or Pancha Koshas and five life breaths or Pancha Praanaas. The letter Bha stands for Bhakti or devotion, ga for Gyan or Jnana or wisdom, va for Vairagya or renunciation, ta for tatwam or realisation and mu for mukthi or liberation. Thus, these five letters represent the progressive steps for man's liberation from bondage or ignorance.

Students! You celebates or Brahmacharis - are the foundation for the mansion of life. The life of a householder may be compared to the walls and that of the recluse or Vaanaprastha, to the roof. If the foundation is not secure, the whole mansion will collapse. Hence you have to develop good qualities, without which there can be no peace for you or for the society. Unfortunately, to-day's man thinks only about himself and his family, ignoring the society. Without the society, where are you and where is your family? This kind of narrow selfishness is prevalent among the so-called devotees also. The devotee thinks about himself and his work first, and about God and His work next, if at all. It is because of this kind of self-centredness that man is unable to enjoy peace or bliss. The Kaurava's formula for life was: "First I, next world and last God. That is why they lost everything, including their lives. On the contrary, the Pandavas' formula was "First God, next world and last I". Hence they came out victorious. There are a number of such instances in our history, which illustrate the prime need to kill the ego.

Students! It is natural for you at this young age to be proud and hasty or impetuous. But true education should result in humility. Sanctify your life, your body, your youth, your time and your actions. Study well and pass with distinction. Make use of your knowledge for the benefit of the society. Recognise that pride and spirituality are the opposite sides of a see-saw. If pride goes up, spirituality goes down and vice versa. It is due to Ahamkaara only that man forgets himself. The greatest and the real bondage is to forget one's own reality. To recognise one's own reality is the true Sakshatkara or realisation. If there is no change in your attitude, all your spiritual practices like Japa, meditation, Yoga, Karma, Seva or service will serve no purpose. It is not the man but the mind that should change. The change of character is more important than the change of clothes.

There are three things you should never forget" "Sathya, Dharma and Nyaaya" - truth, righteousness and justice. Our ancestors were staunch followers of these three principles in their daily lives. But now-days these values are being neglected in India itself, not to speak of the other nations. As future guardians of Indian Culture and tradition, you have to restore these values, by actually putting into practice what you have learnt here during this fortnight. Cultivate love for your country, your culture and your religion. But on no account should you hate or criticise other countries, other cultures, other religions and other persons. Give up narrow-mindedness and cultivate broad-mindedness. Always pray for the welfare of the entire world in accordance with the vedic chanting: "Lokaasamastah Sukhino Bhavantu" - Let all the world be happy.

Develop love for God. Don't give up your devotion to God even if others ridicule you on that account. Don't lose faith in Him when you are in difficulties. Consider every thing - pain and pleasure, loss and gain, joy and sorrow - as God's Prasad - divine gift or grace. Don't forget to chant His Name under any circumstances. God's Name is the only reliable boat to ferry you across the river of life.

Vedic Wisdom

There is no disease equal to greed
There is no enemy greater than anger
There is no sorrow that is greater than poverty
There is no happiness equal to wisdom

Belief in God has declined.
Dharma has disappeared.
Atheism is on the increase.
There is no respect for the Guru-Preceptor.
Devotion to God, respect for our ancient
culture and tradition have been given farewell.
There is no patronage for true education.
Only bread-earning education has become
the order of the day.
These, alas! are the signs of modernity!

"I am in the Light;
The Light is in me;
I am the Light" -

The Jnani who has realised thus will surely become
one with Brahman.

Dear Students!

The Vedic literature is the most ancient in the
world. It is a treasure-house of wisdom. It has contributed
to the all-round development of man. The Veda is the
first-ever book in human history. It is the birth place for
human culture and the basis for all kinds of powers. All
branches of learning have their origin in the Veda. All
Dharmas and virtues have sprung from the Veda. The
Veda is endless, unfathomable, indefinable, and blissful.
The word Veda - is derived from the Sanskrit root Vid -
meaning knowledge or Jnana. Iswara Jnana - knowledge

163

of the Lord - is Veda. Atma-Jnana - knowledge of the Self - is Veda. Brahma-Jnana-Knowledge of the supreme Absolute - is Veda. Adwaita Jnana-Non-dual knowledge - is Veda. Veda is Vijnana- Knowledge *par excellence*. All these terms are synonyms for Self knowledge or Atma-Jnana. The Divinity of the Veda is all-pervasive and has eight aspects of splendour, viz., *Sabda Brahma-mayee* - Sound Brahman, *Charachara mayee* - movable and immovable, Jyotirmayee-Effulgence, *Vaangmayee* - speech and literature, *Nityaananda mayee* - Everlasting Bliss, *Paratpara mayee* - Transcendental, *Maya mayee* - Delusion, and *Sree mayee* - Prosperity. This is indeed the Prajnanamaya Brahma - constant integrated awareness. It does not pertain to one individual, one place or time. It is universal. Knowing that it is not possible for ordinary people to understand such sacred Vedic literature, Sage Vyasa compiled it into four volumes.

The Veda consists of three "kandaas" or Cantos, namely, Karma Kaanda - cantos dealing with rituals and other actions, Upaasana Kaanda - cantos of Devotion, and Jnana Kaanda - Cantos of wisdom. These three divisions represent the progressive steps in man's spiritual evolution. Man starts with actions, recognising that the human body is meant for achieving Dharma - righteousness through Karma. When he goes on performing good karmas, he will in due course become fit for understanding Upaasana - devotional practices. When he worships God over a period of time, with love and in a spirit of dedication, he attains the final stage of Jnana. On the whole, Karma, Upaasana and Jnana may be considered as three stages of one process, comparable to the flower, the raw fruit and the ripe fruit respectively. Since the common people cannot understand and practise the teachings of the Veda, subsidiary literature has been created later in the form of Puranaas - Mythological treatises and Itihaasaas - epics, so that even the lay people can practise Karma, Upaasana and Jnana.

The end of the Veda is Upanishad, which is therefore, called Vedanta. The Upanishads have named the three paths of Karma, Upaasana and Jnana as Yogas. The essence of Karma Yoga is to dedicate all actions to God or to perform all activities as offerings to the Lord, for His pleasure. Upaasana Yoga consists of loving God whole heartedly and with Trikaranasuddhi i.e., harmony and purity of thought, word and deed. It is not true Upaasana if one loves God for the sake of achieving his wordly desires. It should be love for love's sake. The followers of Jnana Yoga consider the whole universe as the manifestation of God. Believing that divinity is residing in all beings in the form of Atma, is called Jnana. Students may wonder how there can be Ekatwa - oneness, when there are so many different forms and names, different kinds of behaviour and different doctrines etc. This doubt can be cleared by considering the example of an ocean. In the fathomless ocean, there are numberless waves. Each wave is different from the other in its size, shape, etc. and it looks as though there is no connection between one wave and another. But a little thinking will reveal to you the fact that they are all different manifestations of one and the same water, and also that they are not different from the ocean. In the same manner, all the different names and forms in the universe are the waves or manifestations of the one and the same ocean of Sat-Chit-Ananda - Existence -Awareness-Bliss. Hence the essence of all the manifested beings is only Sat-Chit-Aanda, despite the superficial or apparent differences in names and forms and their behaviour.

The Bhagavad Gita, which came later into existence, is the essence of the Upanishads. However, it deals with the path of Karma, Upaasana and Jnana in three Shatkas, each Shatka comprising six chapters, thus making up the total of eighteen chapters in the Gita. The first Shatka deals with the path of Karma, the second one with the path of Upaasana and the third one with the path of Jnana. To sum up, the Veda gave rise to the Upanishads, which in turn gave rise to the Bhagavad Gita which serves as a practical guide for human conduct. The Bhagavadgita is not the property or monopoly of the Indians. It is the word of God and is therefore, a universal scripture. There is only one God for all, although there may be different religions and different names and forms of God. In whatever name and form one may worship, it reaches the one and only God. There is only one sun. There are no separate suns like American Sun, British sun, Chinese sun, Indian sun, Pakstani sun and so on. Each country may see the sun at a different time. Just because all of them cannot see the sun at the same time, it will be foolish to think that there are different suns for different countries.

Vedas have very vast, profound and deep meanings. The Gurus or preceptors of ancient times used to adopt stern measures and enforce strict discipline while teaching the Vedas to their students. That is why the Vedas have survived till to-day, successfully withstanding the onslaught of time. Actually, the Vedas are not books in the usual sense of that term. No one claims authorship for them. They are called strutis or knowledge acquired through hearing. Since time immemorial, the Vedas have been coming down through a succession of Gurus and disciples through the process of hearing. The Gurus used to utter the mantras with particular intonations which were prescribed for the purpose and scrupulously followed by the disciples. The Gurus of those days were self-less, pure-hearted and overflowing with love for their students, but unsparing in the matter of discipline among the students. The students too were generally observing the required discipline very scrupulously. If any one disobeyed the master, he would be summarily dismissed from attending the classes. The Gurus would never tolerate any student who was guilty of one or more of the *Akaara Panchaka Arishtas* or the five transgressions beginning with the letter 'A;, viz., Alakshyam - negligence, Avinayam - disobedience, Ahamkaaram - ego, Asooya - jealousy and Asabhyata - lack of social etiquette.

Vysampayana was the foremost among the disciples who learnt the Vedas from the Sage Vyasa. Vysampayana sanctified his life by implicitly obeying his Guru and by learning his lessons studiously and thoroughly. After completing his studies, Vysampayana established a Gurukula - for teaching the Veda to his disciples. By Gurukula - is not meant a separate institution with its own set of rules and regulations like the present day schools and colleges. The Guru's house itself constituted the Gurukula. Whatever kind of food the Guru ate, was given to the disciple as Prasad - holy food. The disciple should stay with the Guru day and night. One disciple by name Yajnavalkya joined Vysampayana's Gurukul. He had a keen intellect and could learn his lessons very fast. The guru was also highly pleased with him. People who knew Yajnavalkya began praising him with the result that he developed Ahamkaram - ego, followed gradually by alakshyam - indifference, and Asabhyata -lack of decorum. Vysampayaan noticed these lapses on the part of Yajnavalkya. One day he called him and told him sternly, "Yajnavalkya! You dont' deserve to stay in this Gurukul any longer. You must leave this place immediately. Before you leave, you must return all that you have learnt from me". Accordingly, Yajnavalkya, who recognised his own shortcomings, vomitted all that he had learnt from his guru. His vomittings were eaten by Tittiri birds and the latter began chanting the Uapnishad which was therefore named as Taittireeya Upanishad.

There are two traditions or Sampradayas in the Veda, viz., Brahma Sampradaya and Aditya Sampradaya. That which was vomitted by Yajnavalkya came to be known as the Brahma Sampradaya, also called the Krishna Yajurveda. After leaving the Gurukul of Vysampayana, Yajnavalkya sincerely repented for his delinquency and atoned for it by giving up food and drink and practised Suryopasaana - Sun worship - undergoing severe austerities by way of penance. Pleased with this penance, the Sun-God appeared before him in the form of Vaaji, and told him, "My child! What is past is past. You should guard yourself against such lapses in future. Betraying the Guru or God is highly dangerous. Be careful hereafter. I will now teach you the Vedas again". So saying the Sun-God taught him the Vedas. The reason for the Sun appearing in the form of Vaaji was that Yajnavalkya's fore-fathers always used to do Anna Dana - free distrbution of food, and therefore their family got the name Vaajasam. The Veda taught by him was also called by the alternative names of Sukla Yajurveda, Vaajasaskandha and Aditya Khanda. Yajurveda has been divided into two. For this reason, although the Vedas were originally four in number, they have subsequently become five, namely Rigveda, Krishna Yajurveda, Sukla Yajurveda, Saama Veda and Atharvana Veda, Recognising that the Sun appeared before him as Vaaji and taught him the Vedas, because of the free distribution of food by his ancestors, Yajnavalkya gave primary importance to Anna-daana in his teaching which, among others, included the following: -

"There is no gift higher than the gift of food and no God higher than the parents. There is no truth higher than Japa and Tapa - reciting the holy Name and doing penance. There is no Dharma higher than compassion and no gain higher than the company of the good. There is no enemy more dangerous than anger and no disease more serious than indebtedness. There is no death more horrible than ill-fame and no wealth more valuable than fame. There is no ornament more beautiful than Smaran-remembering God through chanting His names". Yajnavalkya, moreover, emphasised specially in his teachings to his disciples the extreme importance of service to parents and Guru, as well as Annadaanam - free distribution of food.

Students! we began these classes on the holy Ekadasi day- eleventh day of the lunar fortnight. and we are also concluding the classes on this Ekadasi day. Hence you should consider all these classes as Ekadasi Vratam - observance of the vows of Ekadasi. During the fortnight you have had the valuable opportunity of listening to the lectures form highly distinguished speakers, with rich experience behind them. What they taught you with whole-hearted zeal and enthusiasm, you have listened carefully with much interest and faith. But what is more important than listening, is to put into practice at least some of the things you have learnt and thereby to set an example for others to follow.

You must always remember the five life-breaths relating to the Vedas, which I mentioned earlier. You should avoid these five things: 1) Indifference to what the Guru, parents and other elders teach you 2) Disobedience to the aforesaid, 3) Ahamkaaram - ego 4) Jealousy or envy towards those who are better off, 5) violating the social etiquette or decorum.

Students! What has been taught to you during these fifteen days is the essence of the sacred Vedanta. What has been given to you is the nectar obtained by the churning of all the holy scriptures - Shastras, Puranas and Ithihasas. You are the future leaders, pleaders, and patrons of Mother India. You should lead exemplary lives, treading the path of Sathya and Dharma - truth and righteousness. Under no circumstances should you deviate from this ideal path. Let your secular education go hand in hand with spiritual education.

The Vedas have taught about two kinds of Dharma: Vihita Dharma and Nishiddha Dharma - prescribed Dharma and prohibited Dharma; in other words, the Do's and Don'ts for regulating one's life. Unfortunately, today the prescribed things are being given up, and the prohibited things are being taken up. This is sheer folly and ignorance. The prohibited things should be rejected, even though you might have taken lot of trouble to acquire them. For instance, you have purchased from the market a big mango fruit for five rupees. Just because you have spent five rupees on it, will you eat the skin outside and the stone inside the fruit? No, no. You will eat only the pulp and reject both the skin and stone. Similarly , this world is like a fruit, and you have to accept what is good in it and reject what is bad for you.

Students! You are highly fortunate. Even though there are several millions of people in the world, is it not your exceedingly good luck that only you, who are but a few hundreds in number, have been able to get the benefit of this golden opportunity? However, the purpose of this Summer Course will be served only if at least some of you stand as exemplars to others. You may take up any job, business or agriculture, and occupy any position in your life, but it is extremely important that you do not lose self-confidence while discharging your duties. Lack of Self-confidence is the main cause for all the present-day problems like foul-play, injustice, losses, failures, sorrow and pain. People do not believe in themselves, not to speak of believing others. First of all, develop Self-confidence and that in turn will give you self-satisfaction. Without self-satisfaction, you cannot have contentment. Once you have gained self-satisfaction, then automatically you will be ready for self-sacrifice. Needless to say, where there is self-sacrifice, there will be Self-realisation naturally.

Every student should undertake Satkarmaas - good actions which lead to Chittasuddhi - purity of mind. Where there is purity, there will be Jnana Siddhi - dawn of wisdom. These are all within yourself only. You need not search for them anywhere outside. In this connection, let us consider the example of the wall-clock over there. It has three hands to indicate seconds, minutes and hours respectively. There are sixty points, and twelve hours marked along the circumference of the clock. When the second-hand moves across all the sixty points, the minute-hand moves by only one point. When the minute hand moves over sixty points or the full circumference, the hour-hand moves by only one hour-mark or one-twelfth of the circumference. Now, the second-hand may be compared to our actions. If a large number of good actions are done, the minute-hand which represents Chitta Suddhi - the purity of mind will move by one point. Chittasuddhi is the stage of Upaasana when one engages himself in loving God and worshipping Him in various ways over a period of time leading to Atma-Viswaasam - Self-confidence which represents the hour-hand. The perceptible movements of the second-hand and the minute-hand should bring about the imperceptibly slow movement of the hour-hand. Otherwise no purpose is served by the second-hand and minute-hand. So also, unless your good actions, worship and love of God- lead to Atmaviswas or Self-confidence, the former two will be futile.

Whenever you have time, it will suffice if you take up at least one of the nine modes of Bhakti (such as Sravanam, Kirtanam etc., already explained to you in My earlier discourses). God does not consider how wealthy or how leaned you are; He is concerned only with the sincerity and purity of your mind and heart and about how whole-hearted and genuine your love is. Valmiki was a hunter. Nanda was an untouchable. Kuchela was a pauper. Dhruva and Prahalada were mere lads of five years. Sabari was a tribal woman, illiterate and uncivilised. But all of them had won God's Grace in abundance, because of their whole-hearted devotion, love and surrender. Follow the example of Sabari who always thought of Sri Rama and His happiness, and dedicated all her thoughts, words and deeds to Him alone, so much so that every action of hers was transformed and sublimated into the highest Tapas - penance. From her example, you must learn the lesson that mediation, does not mean sitting idle in a particular posture of the body, as if you are posing for a photograph. As in her case your entire life must become a continuous meditation wherever you may be staying and whatever you may be doing. Whatever you eat or drink must be offered to God as Naivedya or holy offering. In this manner, if you offer everything to the

Lord, you will naturally be prevented from engaging yourself in bad actions or evil ways in your life. Therefore, Students! I am bringing My long discourse to a close, with the hope and blessing that you will practice with your hands what you have heard here through your ears, and thereby sanctify your lives and also contribute your share to make the future of Bharat bright and prosperous.

LIST OF OTHER PUBLICATIONS
SRI SATHYA SAI BOOKS & PUBLICATIONS TRUST, PRASANTHI NILAYAM, A.P. 515 134

ENGLISH

Vahini Series

	Rs. Ps.
Bhagavatha Vahini	11.00
Dharma Vahini	7.00
Dhyana Vahini	5.00
Geeta Vahini	15.50
Jnana Vahini	6.00
Leela Kaivalya Vahini	4.50
Prasanthi Vahini	6.00
Prasnothara Vahini	5.00
Prema Vahini	6.00
Rama Katha Rasa Vahini I	13.00
Rama Katha Rasa Vahini II	11.00
Sandeha Nivarini	6.50
Sathya Sai Vahini	11.50
Sutra Vahini	5.00
Upanishad Vahini	7.00
Vidya Vahini	7.00

Sathya Sai Speaks Series

Sathya Sai Speaks Volume - I	10.00
Sathya Sai Speaks Volume - II	11.00
Sathya Sai Speaks Volume - III	13.00
Sathya Sai Speaks Volume - IV	16.00
Sathya Sai Speaks Volume - V	15.00
Sathya Sai Speaks Volume - VI	15.00
Sathya Sai Speaks Volume - VII A	11.00
Sathya Sai Speaks Volume - VII B	11.00
Sathya Sai Speaks Volume - VIII	13.50
Sathya Sai Speaks Volume - IX	13.50
Sathya Sai Speaks Volume - X	10.50
Sathya Sai Speaks Volume - XI	13.00

Sathyam Sivam Sundaram Series

Sathyam Sivam Sundaram I	10.00
Sathyam Sivam Sundaram II	13.00

		Rs. Ps.
Sathyam Sivam Sundaram III		11.00
Sathyam Sivam Sundaram IV		12.00

Summer Showers Series

Summer Showers in Brindavan	1972	11.00
Summer Showers in Brindavan	1973	13.50
Summer Showers in Brindavan	1974	12.00
Summer Roses on the Blue Mountains	1976	8.50
Summer Showers in Brindavan	1977	11.00
Summer Showers in Brindavan	1978	11.50
Summer Showers in Brindavan	1979	8.50
Summer Showers in Brindavan	1990	14.00

Other Books

Africa for Sai Baba	2.50
Chinna Katha	10.00
Conversations with Bhagawan Sri Sathya Sai Baba *– John S. Hislop*	9.00
Daily Prayers to Bhagawan	5.00
Divine Memories of Sathya Sai Baba *– Diana Baskin*	30.00
Easwaramma the Chosen Mother	7.00
Finding God - *Charles Penn*	30.00
Garland of 108 Precious Gems	6.00
Golden Jubilee Book of Thoughts	25.00
Guide to Indian Culture and Spirituality	6.00
Information Booklet - 1991	3.00
My Baba and I - *John S. Hislop*	18.50
My Beloved - *Charles Penn*	25.00
Namasmarana	4.50
Prasanthi Pathway to Peace	6.50
Sadhana the Inward Path	10.50
Sai Baba the Holy man and the Psychiatrist - *Delox Edn.*	35.00
Sai Baba the Ultimate Experience - *Phyllis Krystall*	24.00
Sathya Sai Baba - God Incarnate	17.00
Sathya Sai Education in Human Values	14.00
Sai Ram - *Charles Penn*	25.00
Spirit and the Mind - *Samuel H. Sandweiss*	30.00
Stories for Children Part I	
Stories for Children Part II	

175

Sathya Sai Lyrics - *Dr. V.K. Gokak*	7.50
Sai Baba Man of Miracles - *Howard Murphet*	28.00
Sai Baba Avatar - *Howard Murphet*	36.00
Sai Baba Invitation to Glory - *Howard Murphet*	24.00

Books are despatched only by Registered Post and not by V.P.P., subject to availability, when indents and remittance are received by Money Order or Bank Draft in favour of The Convenor, Sri Sathya Sai Books and Publications Trust, Prasanthi Nilayam, Anantapur District, A.P., Pin Code 515 134.

Postage (Inland) - Registration charges for each packet (2 Kg. or less) are Rs. 6/- excluding postage charges. Registration charges should be added in calculating the total amount to be remitted to the Convenor.

Postage (Overseas):

Sea Mail despatch: Rs. 52/- (including Registration charges) for each 2 Kg. or less packet.

Air Mail despatch: Rs. 200/- (including Registration charges) for each 2 Kg. or less packet.

SANATHANA SARATHI, our monthly magazine in English and Telugu devoted to the moral and spiritual uplift of humanity through Sathya, Dharma, Shanthi, Prema is being published regularly.

Annual Subscription (Inland)		Rs. 20.00
-do-	Overseas Air Mail	Rs. 140.00
-do-	Overseas Sea Mail	70.00

to be remitted to – THE CONVENOR, SRI SATHYA SAI BOOKS AND PUBLICATIONS TRUST, PRASANTHI NILAYAM P.O., ANANTAPUR DISTRICT, A.P., PIN CODE 515 134.